Vegetarian
COOKER–TOP
COOKERY

Quick and Easy Meat-Free Meals

by

Pamela Brown

Illustrated by Kim Blundell

THORSONS PUBLISHERS LIMITED
Wellingborough, Northamptonshire

*Published in co-operation with
The Vegetarian Society of the United Kingdom Ltd.*

First published 1978
This edition revised and reset March 1985
Second Impression June 1985

British Library Cataloguing in Publication Data

Brown, Pamela
   Vegetarian cooker-top cookery.
   1. Vegetarian cookery
   I. Title   II. Brown, Pamela
   Vegetarian cooker-top cookery
   641.5'636   TX837

ISBN 0-7225-1129-9

Printed in Great Britain by
Richard Clay (The Chaucer Press) Ltd,
Bungay, Suffolk

Vegetarian COOKER-TOP COOKERY

A vegetarian cookbook with a difference, designed specially for cooking delicious, wholesome meals without using an oven.

CONTENTS

INTRODUCTION

This book is for you if you ever need to prepare a good meal without the use of an oven.

You may — like me — be fortunate in having all the facilities of a first-class kitchen, but you do not want to waste fuel by heating a whole oven for just one meal. I believe that when the oven goes on it should always be used to full capacity.

This book is for you if you live in a bed-sit with one ring (there are specially devised menus for one-ring cooking), and it is for you if you cook in a caravan, a boat or outdoors.

It is also for you if you are going on a self-catering holiday because not only do the recipes save on fuel, but they also take little time to prepare and cook. The fact that this is a no-meat cookery book is particularly useful for holidaymakers abroad where the meat available can be doubtful!

Readers unfamiliar with vegetarian food need have no fears that any essential food value is missing. Protein is found in nuts, cheese, eggs and milk, as well as in vegetables, whole grains and pulses. The important word is 'whole', and this means grains that have not been processed and have their outside skins intact, and flour that has been milled in its entirety with nothing removed.

The recipes in this book have been designed for these foods. Unless otherwise stated, flour means wholemeal flour. If at first it seems too coarse you can sieve out the bran, but be sure to use it elsewhere: some recipes specifically include bran. When a 'white sauce' is made with wholemeal flour it has a real taste to it, and it is not just a vehicle for other added flavours.

It is my aim to show you how to make the best of straightforward fresh wholefoods. You will not need to hunt for exotic fruit or vegetables to make any of the recipes. All you need to do is to find a shop that sells wholefoods and, if you don't grow your own vegetables, make sure that the ones you buy are really fresh.

Herbs and spices need to be fresh too, and they should be bought in small quantities. Herbs make such a difference to taste that — even if you only have a bed-sit — you should grow a few for yourself. Basil, parsley, mint, thyme, rosemary and sage are all possibilities. If you do have to use dried herbs — be sparing.

Where salt and pepper are included, quantities are rarely given as this is so much a matter of taste. Sea salt and freshly ground black pepper are best. Butter is rarely mentioned because it is high in saturated fats, and eggs are used sparingly for the same reason (see introduction to egg recipes). There are plenty of acceptable margarines available.

Although most cooks will want to start by following each recipe exactly, variations should be tried. In a busy life it is not always easy to shop for specific items, and it is fun to try out new things — always of course keeping the balance right. My own home-cooking tends to depend on what provisions are in stock that approximate to the recipe.

The salad section is quite small but it is very important as it is good practice to eat some raw food every day. Any amount of combinations of raw fruit and vegetables can be worked out — and they are often very good with hot food.

Equipment is also important, and I have devoted a short section to it. If you are short on space you will need to take particular care in choosing the best for your purpose.

Cooking is about enjoyment — so I hope you will have fun using the recipes in this book and that you will give pleasure to those who eat the results of your efforts.

Unless otherwise stated all recipes make enough for at least four people.

1.

USEFUL EQUIPMENT

There are few essentials needed for vegetarian cookery. You do need several good knives; a chopping board; and two graters — one for raw vegetables and cheese and one for nuts. Then, apart from the usual wooden spoons, frying pans, saucepans, bowls, etc., you need a sieve, and the best to choose is the *mouli*-sieve with a handle (see illustration).

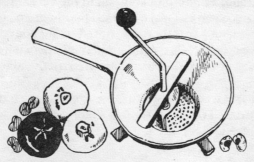

Figure 1. Mouli-sieve

A liquidizer or blender I would place very high on the list of desirables. You can cut down the work of soup and sauce making and if you buy a liquidizer which incorporates a coffee grinder you will be able to reduce nuts to a powder and make quick breadcrumbs, etc. There is quite a selection — choose the sturdiest and largest that you can afford.

A double steamer saves space and cooks conservatively — retaining all the goodness of the vegetables. I much prefer the Chinese bamboo rings as illustrated. You can buy them to fit standard saucepans, and they fit tightly on to each other, so several can be put on to one saucepan.

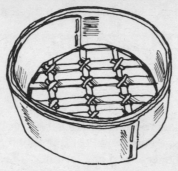

Figure 2.   Bamboo steaming ring

A pressure cooker will probably add to the versatility of cooker-top cookery since you can make steamed puddings and savouries in a short time without filling the room with steam for hours. It of course cuts down the time for all cooking — although there is a danger that food may be over-cooked unless times are strictly adhered to.

A griddle makes it much easier to make scones, and even bread rolls without an oven. The flat surface is slightly raised from the heat ensuring an even distribution.

Figure 3.   A griddle

A Chinese wok is by no means essential, but its inverted dome shape allows minimum cooking of vegetables by stir frying, and then they can be pushed up the sides to keep hot while the rest of the food is being cooked. This stands slightly away from the heat (see illustration).

Figure 4. Chinese Wok

A slow-cooker is an earthenware casserole that sits in a container heated by electricity. The initial expense is quite high but very little electricity is used and the advantage is that food cooks for a long time very slowly. I have included a few recipes specifically for a slow-cooker since they are becoming more popular and are particularly useful for the cook with restricted cooking equipment.

Figure 5. A slow-cooker

A food muff is simply a very large cosy (like a tea cosy). It needs to be large enough to take a saucepan, which sits in an insulated 'nest' with the cosy on top. Something that could be very easily home-made.

Figure 6.   A food muff

2.

BREAD, SCONES AND OATCAKES

The lack of an oven does not mean that you are deprived of home-made bread and scones.

The griddle can be used for bread rolls as well as scones and cakes. If you do not have a griddle you can use a good strong clean frying pan — but you will need to see that the heat is evenly distributed, and keep watch for signs of sticking.

CHAPATIS

Imperial (Metric)	American
½ lb (225g) wholemeal flour	2 cupsful wholewheat flour
½ teaspoonful sea salt	½ teaspoonful sea salt
7½ fl oz (215ml) water (approx.)	¾ cupful water (approx.)
2 oz (55g) extra flour for kneading	½ cupful extra flour for kneading

1. Mix flour and salt, make a well in the centre, and fork in water to make a soft dough.

2. Sprinkle flour on to a board, and knead the dough for at least 5 minutes (this can be done using the dough hook of an electric mixer).

3. Sprinkle water over the dough, cover with a damp cloth and leave for at least half an hour.

4. Knead again for another 5 minutes. Divide dough into 10-12 pieces, flatten them out into thin circles with a 5 inch (12cm) diameter, still using extra flour to make sure they are not sticky.

5. Grease the griddle and cook until underside is done — slightly browned — then turn, and with a cloth press down all round edges to make centre puff up. Then serve immediately.

DROP SCONES

Imperial (Metric)	American
Squeeze of lemon juice	Squeeze of lemon juice
½ pint (285ml) milk (buttermilk is best)	1⅓ cupsful milk (buttermilk is best)
½ lb (225g) wholemeal self-raising flour	2 cupsful wholewheat self-raising flour
2 tablespoonsful raw cane sugar	2 tablespoonsful raw cane sugar
½ teaspoonful cream of tartar	½ teaspoonful cream of tartar
1 egg	1 egg

1. Incorporate the lemon juice with milk (not needed if buttermilk is used).

2. Sift dry ingredients — make well in centre and mix in lightly beaten egg with enough milk to make a thick batter.

3. Drop in neat spoonsful on to a moderately hot griddle. When bubbles cover top, turn and cook other side. Serve buttered — good with a little treacle.

GRIDDLE SCONES

Imperial (Metric)
½ lb (225g) plain wholemeal flour (sieve out bran if you wish to lighten)
½ teaspoonful bicarbonate of soda
½ teaspoonful cream of tartar
¼ teaspoonful sea salt
Plain unsweetened yogurt

American
2 cupsful wholewheat flour (sieve out bran if you wish to lighten)
½ teaspoonful baking soda
½ teaspoonful cream of tartar
¼ teaspoonful sea salt
Plain unsweetened yogurt

1. Mix dry ingredients by sieving together, then add just enough yogurt to make a soft pliable dough.

2. Turn on to floured board, divide into four, form into rounds then cut each into quarters about ½ inch (1cm) thick.

3. Have a moderately hot griddle (test by putting a little flour on, if it browns quickly it is too hot; it should take several minutes to brown). Put the well-floured scones on the griddle, when risen and brownish underneath (about 5 minutes) turn and do the other side. Specially good warm with butter or margarine — a nut butter is excellent.

OATCAKES

Imperial (Metric)
4 oz (115g) medium oatmeal
2 oz (55g) wholemeal flour
¼ teaspoonful bicarbonate of soda
¼ teaspoonful sea salt
1 tablespoonful melted white
   vegetable fat or nut fat
Approx. 3 tablespoonsful hot water

American
1 cupful medium oatmeal
½ cupful wholewheat flour
¼ teaspoonful baking soda
¼ teaspoonful sea salt
1 tablespoonful melted white
   vegetable fat or nut fat
Approx. 3 tablespoonsful hot water

1. Mix all dry ingredients in a bowl, make a well in the centre and pour in melted fat and enough hot water to make a stiff dough.

2. Form into a ball, then taking about a quarter at a time knead mixture on well-floured board until it is thin and flat.

3. Transfer to moderately hot griddle and cook both sides. The old way was to cook one side then toast the other before a bright fire.

SOFT BREAD ROLLS

Imperial (Metric)
½ oz (15g) dried yeast
1 teaspoonful raw cane sugar, or
   honey
½ pint (285ml) warm water, or a
   little more
15 oz (425g) strong wholemeal flour
1 oz (30g) soya flour
½ teaspoonful sea salt
1 tablespoonful corn oil

American
1 tablespoonful dried yeast
1 teaspoonful raw cane sugar, or
   honey
1⅓ cupful warm water, or a little
   more
3¾ cupsful strong wholewheat flour
¼ cupful soy flour
½ teaspoonful sea salt
1 tablespoonful corn oil

1. Add yeast and sugar to half the warm water, stir and leave for about 10 minutes or until it is frothy on top.

2. Mix flours and salt in a bowl, make well in centre and pour in yeast mixture. Then put the oil in the basin that held the yeast,

rinse round, add this to flour. Pour the rest of liquid into the basin, rinse round and add a little more to flour. Mix to a soft elastic dough adding more water if necessary.

3. Knead until smooth, then set aside (preferably inside oiled plastic bag with room to rise).

4. When double in bulk gently knead again. Cut into small pieces, roll each into flat rounds and set aside again for 15 minutes.

5. Heat griddle, flour bread rolls before putting on griddle, then cook as for Griddle Scones (page 15).

3.

CHEESE

Cheese is high in protein and some vitamins and it makes a satisfying meal. There are so many varieties of cheese that the recipes can be altered by simply substituting one for another, and it is well worth doing this. Remember that cheese must be heated slowly, if it gets hot too quickly it becomes tough and unpalatable.

BROCCOLI CHEESE

Imperial (Metric)

½ lb (225g) broccoli, lightly cooked

½ pint (285ml) thick Tangy Cheese Sauce (made with slightly less milk than recipe on page 66)

½ a tinned red pepper, cut in strips

A few stuffed olives, sliced

1 oz (30g) grated cheese (Gouda is good)

1 oz (30g) wholemeal bread — cut in dice and soaked in 1 egg, beaten

Oil for frying

American

½ pound broccoli, lightly cooked

1⅓ cupsful thick Tangy Cheese Sauce (made with slightly less milk than recipe on page 66)

½ a canned red pepper, cut in strips

A few stuffed olives, sliced

¼ cupful grated cheese (Gouda is good)

1 slice wholewheat bread — cut in dice and soaked in 1 egg, beaten

Oil for frying

1.   Put the cooked broccoli into a flameproof dish and pour over the hot sauce. Arrange strips of pepper on top with olive slices, sprinkle with grated cheese and put under moderate grill.

2.   While this is browning fry the soaked bread cubes in hot oil.

3.   Scatter the bread croûtons over the broccoli before serving.

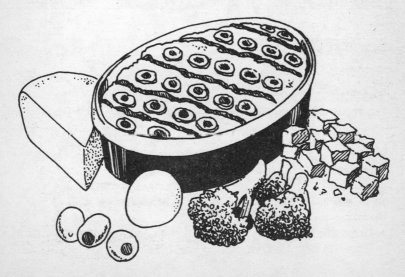

CHEESE AIGRETTES

Imperial (Metric)
1 oz (30g) vegetable margarine
¼ pint (140ml) water
2½ oz (70g) wholemeal flour
2 small eggs
2 oz (55g) Cheddar cheese (grated)
Sea salt
Freshly ground black pepper
Cayenne pepper
Mustard

American
2½ tablespoonsful vegetable
  margarine
⅔ cupful water
⅝ cupful wholewheat flour
2 small eggs
½ cupful Cheddar cheese (grated)
Sea salt
Freshly ground black pepper
Cayenne pepper
Mustard

1. Boil margarine and water, then add the flour and beat until smooth
   — cool.

2. Add eggs, beating well, then add cheese, salt and pepper and
   a pinch of cayenne, and mustard.

3. Drop small spoonfuls into hot fat, it should not brown them too
   quickly.

4. When the aigrettes are golden and crisp drain on kitchen paper.

CHEESE MUFF
Serves 1

Imperial (Metric)
1 egg beaten with 1 tablespoonful
  milk
A little butter and seasoning
2 oz (55g) of a good tasty cheese,
  finely grated
Some made-up mild mustard
Slice of wholemeal toast

American
1 egg beaten with 1 tablespoonful
  milk
A little butter and seasoning
½ cupful of a good tasty cheese,
  finely grated
Some made-up mild mustard
Slice of wholewheat toast

1. Scramble the egg then add grated cheese and seasoning, stir and
   leave on heat long enough to combine.

2. Pile on to hot toast which has been spread with a little mustard. Also good with mashed potatoes and peas.

CHEESE PUFFS

Imperial (Metric)
¼ pint (140ml) milk
1 large egg
2 oz (55g) wholemeal flour
2 oz (55g) cheese, grated
1 oz (30g) fresh breadcrumbs
Sea salt
Freshly ground black pepper
Pinch dry mustard
Dash *Holbrook's* Worcester sauce
1 tablespoonful parsley, well
  chopped

American
⅔ cupful milk
1 large egg
½ cupful wholewheat flour
½ cupful cheese, grated
½ cupful fresh breadcrumbs
Sea salt
Freshly ground black pepper
Pinch dry mustard
Dash vegetarian Worcester sauce
1 tablespoonful parsley, well
  chopped

1. Beat milk and egg into flour, add all other ingredients.

2. Drop in spoonfuls on greased frying pan or griddle. Turn when underside is cooked. Serve hot.

CHEESE AND SPINACH GRILL

Imperial (Metric)	American
½ oz (15g) vegetable margarine	1¼ tablespoonsful vegetable margarine
1 lb (455g) spinach (or swiss chard or ruby chard)	1 pound spinach (or swiss chard or ruby chard)
Pinch sea salt	Pinch sea salt
2 eggs, beaten	2 eggs, beaten
1 teaspoonful mustard	1 teaspoonful mustard
2 tomatoes, skinned and sliced	2 tomatoes, skinned and sliced

1. Melt margarine in pan, add the chopped spinach with a pinch of sea salt. Toss, cook over low heat with closed lid, taking care not to burn.

2. When cooked, chop finely.

3. Add beaten eggs, stir over heat for 1 minute, mix in half of the cheese and mustard.

4. Put into a greased, shallow flameproof dish, arrange sliced tomatoes over the top and sprinkle over rest of cheese.

5. Put under moderate grill until cheese bubbles.

NO COOK KEBABS

You need long kebab skewers for this, or do short ones on orange sticks.

Have several different cheeses — for instance a strong blue, milder Edam and mature Cheddar. Cut them into squares and triangles.

Alternate cheeses with any variety of foods, such as green and black grapes, dates, juicy raisins, pineapple chunks, tomato quarters, orange segments, gherkins, olives, red and green pepper strips and so on.

Serve the kebabs with salads — or they can be put under the grill for a minute or two just to start melting the cheese.

ROBIN'S FAVOURITE

Just about the simplest way to serve cheese is to grate a good portion over mashed potatoes with baked beans. Grating seems to give cheese an extra flavour, and of course more or less all children love baked beans!

4.
CONVENIENCE FOODS

There are times when tinned food is useful, so here are a few ideas for making interesting meals using the tinned savouries that are available.

It is worth experimenting with different makes and varieties. I find people react in surprising ways to all of them — it is very much a question of individual taste.

APPLE AND GINGER SAVOURY

Imperial (Metric)
1 tablespoonful oil
1 medium tart apple, diced
2 tablespoonsful crystallized ginger, chopped
1 tin savoury nutmeat, diced fairly small, or left over home-made nut savoury
1 vegetable bouillon in a little hot water
Sea salt and freshly ground black pepper

American
1 tablespoonful oil
1 medium sharp apple, diced
2 tablespoonsful crystallized ginger, chopped
1 can savoury nutmeat, diced fairly small, or left over home-made nut savoury
1 vegetable bouillon in a little hot water
Sea salt and freshly ground black pepper

1. Heat oil in a large saucepan.

2. Add diced apple and ginger, shake gently for 1 minute.

3. Add nutmeat, shake over flame for another minute.

4. Add bouillon dissolved in hot water, and seasoning, stir carefully, cook with lid on just until apple is cooked through.

5. Serve with rice or potatoes and green vegetable or side salad.

CORN AND NUTMEAT PANCAKES

Imperial (Metric)
4 heaped tablespoons wholemeal
    flour
1 tablespoonful oil
Water
Sea salt and freshly ground black
    pepper
1 egg white
1 small tin savoury nutmeat
3 oz (85g) sweetcorn (frozen or
    tinned)
Oil for frying

American
4 heaped tablespoons wholewheat
    flour
1 tablespoonful oil
Water
Sea salt and freshly ground black
    pepper
1 egg white
1 small can savoury nutmeat
½ cupful sweetcorn (frozen or
    canned)
Oil for frying

1. Make a batter by combining flour with oil and enough water
    to make thick dropping consistency, then season.

2. Whip egg white stiffly, fold it in to the batter.

3. Gently fork in nutmeat and sweetcorn.

4. Drop in spoonsful into hot shallow fat, turn after a few minutes.
    Good with vegetables or salad.

NUTMEAT FRITTERS

Imperial (Metric)
1 small onion, finely chopped
1 small parsnip, grated
Oil for frying
Water
1 small tin any kind of nutmeat or
    vegetarian 'sausages'
1 egg
1 tablespoonful tomato ketchup (or
    similar)
Few drops *Tabasco*
Bran, breadcrumbs or sesame seeds

American
1 small onion, finely chopped
1 small parsnip, grated
Oil for frying
Water
1 small can any kind of nutmeat or
    vegetarian 'sausages'
1 egg
1 tablespoonful tomato catsup (or
    similar)
Few drops *Tabasco*
Bran, breadcrumbs or sesame seeds

1. Sauté onion and parsnip in a little oil in a saucepan.

2. Add a little water and cook with closed lid until soft.

3. Mash nutmeat and beat in the egg.

4. Gradually add cooked vegetables to nutmeat mixture and beat in ketchup and *Tabasco*.

5. Spread on to a plate and cool for a few minutes then shape into small flat discs, dip in bran or similar and fry in shallow fat.

Note: For a crisper finish coat with egg before dipping in bran. Good with tomato or mushroom sauce and cooked vegetables, or with salad.

SOSMIX FLATTIES

Imperial (Metric)	American
Sosmix or similar dry vegetarian 'sausage' mixture	*Sosmix* or similar dry vegetarian 'sausage' mixture
Sage and onion stuffing	Sage and onion stuffing
Water	Water
Oil for frying	Oil for frying

1. Mix *Sosmix* and stuffing (equal quantities) with water as directed on packet — leave for about five minutes and make sure enough water is used (it is surprising how much is needed!).

2. Form into very thin cakes and fry in shallow fat.

Note: Makes a good breakfast dish with egg and tomato. Try experimenting with other seasonings and herbs to add new flavours to this very useful quick mix powder.

STEAMED PEPPER RISOTTO

Imperial (Metric)	American
2 oz (55g) vegetable margarine	¼ cupful vegetable margarine
1 onion, chopped	1 onion, chopped
1 small tin risotto	1 small can risotto
1 red pepper, seeded and finely chopped	1 red pepper, seeded and finely chopped
1 large stick celery, finely chopped	1 large stalk celery, finely chopped
4 oz (115g) fresh wholemeal breadcrumbs	2 cupful fresh wholewheat breadcrumbs
1 egg	1 egg
Juice of ½ lemon	Juice of ½ lemon
3 tablespoonsful parsley, finely chopped	3 tablespoonsful parsley, finely chopped
Sea salt and freshly ground black pepper	Sea salt and freshly ground black pepper

1. Melt the margarine, add onion and cook for a moment, then add the rest of the ingredients.

2. Put them into a well-greased basin, cover with greased greaseproof paper and then aluminium foil, secure with string or put ¼ inch (5mm) elastic round the top, which is easier to get off.

3. Bring 1½ pints/850ml (3¾ cupsful) water to boil in pressure cooker with trivet in place. Put in risotto and keep on boil over low heat for 5 minutes.

4. Bring to 15 lbs pressure for 10 minutes, reduce at room temperature. Serve hot with green vegetables.

Note: This dish can be steamed in an ordinary steamer, in which case it will require 1 hour.

STUFFED TOMATOES
Serves 1

Imperial (Metric)
2 large tomatoes
2 *Sausalatas* (or similar tinned savoury)
1 tablespoonful lemon and thyme stuffing
Pinch dry mustard
Pinch curry powder
Pinch oregano
Sea salt and freshly ground black pepper
½ egg (optional)
1 tablespoonful grated cheese (optional)

American
2 large tomatoes
2 *Sausalatas* (or similar canned savoury)
1 tablespoonful lemon and thyme stuffing
Pinch dry mustard
Pinch curry powder
Pinch oregano
Sea salt and freshly ground black pepper
½ egg (optional)
1 tablespoonful grated cheese (optional)

1. Halve tomatoes. Scoop out flesh and turn them upside-down to drain.

2. Mash flesh in a bowl, then mix in *Sausalatas*, seasonings, stuffing mixture and egg if used. Add a little water if needed, this will depend on size of tomatoes and whether egg is used.

3. Cook this mixture in a saucepan, stirring all the time until it is heated through.

4. Place filling in tomatoes, top with grated cheese (optional) and put under the grill to heat tomatoes and gently brown cheese.

5. Serve with peas, mushrooms and chipped potatoes.

5.

EGGS

Eggs are high in food value, but they are also high in saturated fats. It is generally agreed that we should eat as few saturated fats as possible: so as egg may often form part of made-up dishes care should be taken not to allow them to feature too often on the menu.

Since eggs do of course make a quick satisfying meal the following recipes have been included to be used now and then.

AUBERGINE EGGS

Imperial (Metric)	American
1 small onion, finely chopped	1 small onion, finely chopped
Oil for frying	Oil for frying
½ aubergine, cut in ½ inch (1cm) slices	½ eggplant, cut in ½ inch slices
1 egg	1 egg
1 tablespoonful milk	1 tablespoonful milk
½ teaspoonful sesame salt	½ teaspoonful sesame salt
A few chopped almonds	A few chopped almonds
Fresh parsley, chopped	Fresh parsley, chopped

1. Fry the onion in the oil for a few minutes, then add aubergine (eggplant) slices, shake to avoid burning, cover pan and cook gently for 5-10 minutes until aubergine (eggplant) is done.

2. Set aubergine (eggplant) and onion into a fairly flat dish and keep warm.

3. Scramble the egg and milk in a separate pan or use the frying pan (this is likely to be more tasty but not such a good colour).

4. Sprinkle aubergine (eggplant) with sesame salt, pile on scrambled egg, sprinkle again with a little more sesame salt and the almonds and parsley. Serve at once.

EGG ENVELOPES

Imperial (Metric)	American
2 oz (55g) mushrooms, sliced	¾ cupful mushrooms, sliced
1 carrot, chopped very fine	1 carrot, chopped very fine
Small bunch of chives	Small bunch of chives
Oil for frying	Oil for frying
A little lemon peel, grated	A little lemon peel, grated
Grate of nutmeg, sea salt and freshly ground black pepper	Grate of nutmeg, sea salt and freshly ground black pepper
4 eggs	4 eggs

1. Sauté the vegetables and chives in oil for 5 minutes, add lemon peel and seasoning, continue to sauté gently until cooked.

2. Beat eggs with a little salt.

3. Grease an omelette pan and place about 2 tablespoons egg in it. When it starts to set place 1 tablespoonful of the vegetable mixture on top. Carefully fold the egg envelope over to seal in mixture.

4. Remove egg envelope onto a plate over hot water, and keep covered until all are done.

STIR-FRIED VEGETABLES WITH EGGS

Preferably use a Chinese wok (see page 11) but a good large frying pan will do.

Take any green vegetables such as cabbage, leek, Brussels sprouts — shred them finely and stir-fry in a little oil in the base of the wok. After a few minutes draw vegetables up the sides, and add some soya sauce, pinch chilli powder, pinch ginger, freshly ground black pepper and celery salt. Cook a few mushrooms in this, stirring all the time, then add some mung beans sprouted, they can be tinned or sprout your own (page 60). Keep stirring until all are nearly cooked, then draw them up sides. Drop eggs in the centre of the wok, gently keep them moving — breaking yolks or not as preferred, then cover until eggs are cooked.

Serve vegetables in a mound with eggs on top . . . very good with a dish of brown rice.

SCOTCH EGGS

Use recipe for *Sosmix* Flatties (page 27) or the
Nut Savoury mixture (page 39).

1. Hard boil 1 egg per person.

2. Shell, sprinkle with a little flour then wrap mixture round. Do
   this by flattening a ball of mixture into a circle shape on a floured
   board and then moulding round the egg.

3. Deep fry. (If it is preferred to shallow fry eggs can be carefully
   cut in half lengthways and mixture wrapped round each half.)

Note: If *Sosmix* is used they are better hot. The nut mixture ones
are also very good cold with salad.

SOUFFLÉ SPANISH OMELETTE

Serves 2

Imperial (Metric)	American
3 large eggs, separated	3 large eggs, separated
3 tablespoonsful milk	3 tablespoonsful milk
Sea salt and fresh ground black pepper	Sea salt and fresh ground black pepper
A little oil	A little oil
6 oz (170g) peas, cooked (or delicious raw if home grown)	1 cupful peas, cooked (or delicious raw if home grown)
1 potato, cooked and diced	1 potato, cooked and diced
6 oz (170g) sweetcorn kernels, cooked	1 cupful sweetcorn kernels, cooked
3 oz (85g) sprouted wheat	½ cupful sprouted wheat

1. Combine the egg yolks and milk, add a little sea salt and freshly ground black pepper.

2. Heat oil in pan, scatter all vegetables in so they are fairly evenly distributed — heat them through.

3. Meanwhile whisk the egg whites until stiff.

4. Fold into the yolk mixture, then put on to vegetables.

5. When the bottom of the omelette is set, put the whole pan under a moderate grill in order to set the top

Note: Add to flavour by sprinkling a little very finely grated cheese over the top of the omelette, and putting it back under the grill for a minute.

6.

NUTS

Nuts are a good source of protein and are versatile. They can, of course, be eaten whole with salad, but they also have many uses when they are chopped, grated, or ground to a fine powder. All the following recipes can be varied by using different kinds and combinations of nuts.

Apart from eating them whole the easiest way to serve nuts is to grate them with a *mouli* grater (which gives a soft consistency but not a powder), then sprinkle over salad or cooked vegetables — this is particularly good over floury boiled potatoes with a good portion of butter or polyunsaturated margarine. In fact this makes a satisfying meal eaten with shredded raw cabbage and grated carrot — ultra simple though it is!

ALMOND PRUNE NOISETTES

Imperial (Metric)
2 oz (55g) prunes, cooked and stoned
4 oz (115g) almonds, finely ground (with skins)
Sesame seeds

American
½ cupful prunes, cooked and stoned
1 cupful almonds, finely ground (with skins)
Sesame seeds

1. Chop the cooked prunes and mix them well with the almonds.

2. Form the mixture into small balls and roll in sesame seeds.

3. Serve on rounds of pineapple or slices of apple (dipped in lemon juice to preserve colour) with salad.

ALMOND AND RYE RISSOLES

Imperial (Metric)
2 oz (55g) almonds, medium ground (with skins)
1 oz (30g) rye flakes
1 tablespoonful sage and onion stuffing
1 egg
Sea salt and freshly ground black pepper
1 tablespoonful vegetarian stock, clear soup or water
Oil for frying

American
½ cupful almonds, medium ground (with skins)
½ cupful rye flakes
1 tablespoonful sage and onion stuffing
1 egg
Sea salt and freshly ground black pepper
1 tablespoonful vegetarian stock, clear soup or water
Oil for frying

1. Mix all ingredients together to make stiffish consistency.

2. Form into rissoles and shallow fry.

BRAZIL NUT CROQUETTES

Imperial (Metric)
4 oz (115g) Brazil nuts, ground
1 oz (30g) sesame seeds
1 oz (30g) bran
1 onion, finely chopped
1 egg
1 teaspoonful sesame salt
A good grate nutmeg
1 teaspoonful grated lemon rind
1 tablespoonful parsley
Oil for frying

American
1 cupful Brazil nuts, ground
⅕ cupful sesame seeds
¼ cupful bran
1 onion, finely chopped
1 egg
1 teaspoonful sesame salt
A good grate nutmeg
1 teaspoonful grated lemon rind
1 tablespoonful parsley
Oil for frying

1. Mix all the ingredients together.

2. Form into flattish cakes.

3. Fry in shallow fat, turning when underside is firm.

4. Serve with hot tomato or cheese sauce and vegetables, or hot with cold salad vegetables.

CASHEW CURRY PANCAKES

Imperial (Metric)	American
1 onion, chopped	1 onion, chopped
4 oz (115g) mushrooms, sliced	1½ cupsful mushrooms, sliced
2 sticks celery, chopped	2 stalks celery, chopped
2 tablespoonsful oil	2 tablespoonsful oil
1 orange	1 orange
4 oz (115g) cashew nuts	¾ cupful cashew nuts
1 teaspoonful curry powder	1 teaspoonful curry powder
1 teaspoonful curry paste	1 teaspoonful curry paste
¼ teaspoonful garam masala	¼ teaspoonful garam masala
1 teaspoonful Muscovado sugar	1 teaspoonful Muscovado sugar
Pancake Batter (page 44)	Pancake Batter (page 44)

1. Sauté onion, mushrooms and celery in oil for a few minutes.

2. Squeeze one half of the orange, put juice and all other ingredients into pan, stir, and simmer, adding a little water if it is too dry, but aiming at a thick mixture.

3. Simmer on very low heat for about 20 minutes.

4. While this is cooking make the pancakes and keep them hot on a plate over a pan of simmering water.

5. Test the mixture for taste, and adjust seasoning then fill the pancakes and serve with orange slices.

CHESTNUT AND CASHEW RISSOLES

Imperial (Metric)	American
2 oz (55g) cashew nuts, medium ground	½ cupful cashew nuts, medium ground
1 oz (30g) millet flakes	¼ cupful millet flakes
Sea salt and freshly ground black pepper	Sea salt and freshly ground black pepper
1 egg	1 egg
Chestnut purée	Chestnut purée
Oil for frying	Oil for frying

1. Mix cashews and millet flakes with a little salt and pepper, add the egg and enough chestnut purée to make a thick mixture.

2. Form into rissole shapes.

3. Shallow fry.

CASHEW MEXICAN MIX

Imperial (Metric)	American
1 large onion, chopped	1 large onion, chopped
Oil for frying	Oil for frying
4 oz (115g) cashew nuts	1 cupful cashew nuts
1 medium tin red kidney beans or soya beans	1 medium can red kidney beans or soy beans
2 cloves garlic, chopped	2 cloves garlic, chopped
Shake of *Tabasco*	Shake of *Tabasco*
Pinch of cayenne	Pinch of cayenne
1 teaspoonful paprika	1 teaspoonful paprika
Sea salt and freshly ground black pepper	Sea salt and freshly ground black pepper
A little water	A little water

1. Sauté onion in oil until softened.

2. Add the rest of the ingredients and simmer for 15 minutes.

NUT SAVOURY — STEAMED

Imperial (Metric)	American
1 large onion, finely chopped	1 large onion, finely chopped
1 large carrot, finely grated	1 large carrot, finely grated
Oil for frying	Oil for frying
6 oz (170g) mixed nuts, ground	1½ cupsful mixed nuts, ground
4 oz (115g) bran	1 cupful bran
2 oz (55g) tvp mince	½ cupful tvp mince
1 egg	1 egg
2 tablespoonsful tomato purée	2 tablespoonsful tomato paste
1 tablespoonful yeast extract	1 tablespoonful yeast extract
Sea salt and freshly ground black pepper	Sea salt and freshly ground black pepper
Dash *Tabasco*, soya sauce or any other ketchup	Dash *Tabasco*, soy sauce or any other catsup
A good sprig of thyme and rosemary, minced	A good sprig of thyme and rosemary, minced
Water or vegetable stock	Water or vegetable stock

1. Sauté the onion and carrot in oil for 5 minutes.

2. Add the rest of the ingredients, using enough liquid to make a sticky consistency.

3. Grease a straight sided container, fill to near the top with the mixture, cover with greased greaseproof paper and aluminium foil.

4. To steam in pressure cooker bring 1½ pints/850ml (3¾ cupsful) water to boil in pressure cooker with trivet in place. Put in the Nut Savoury, and keep on boil over low heat for 5 minutes, then bring to 15 pounds (6 kilos) pressure for 15 minutes. Reduce at room temperature. To steam in the ordinary way this dish will need about 1¼ hours.

5. Serve hot with green vegetables and a sauce or allow to get quite cold and then slice and serve with salad.

NUT SAVOURY — RISSOLES

Ingredients as above

1. Sauté the onion and carrot for 5 minutes.

2. Add all the other ingredients including enough water to make a quite sticky consistency.

3. Simmer over a low heat until the mixture is thick, turn on to a plate and allow to cool.

4. Form into rissole shapes and shallow fry.

Note: These rissoles can be dipped in beaten egg and then breadcrumbs before frying.

NUT FRITTERS

For the batter:

Imperial (Metric)	American
4 heaped tablespoonsful wholemeal flour	4 heaped tablespoonsful wholewheat flour
1 tablespoonful oil	1 tablespoonful oil
Water	Water
Sea salt and freshly ground black pepper	Sea salt and freshly ground black pepper
1 egg white	1 egg white
1 quantity rissole or croquette mixture shaped into small fritters	1 quantity rissole or croquette mixture, shaped into small fritters
Deep oil for frying	Deep oil for frying

1. Make a batter by combining flour with oil and enough water to be a very thick consistency, then season.

2. Whisk egg white stiffly and fold it in to the batter.

3. Carefully coat each rissole in turn and drop into hot fat. The batter will puff out and care should be taken not to brown it too much.

4.   Drain on kitchen paper and serve with green vegetables.

TOASTED NUT DIP

Imperial (Metric)
1 teaspoonful paprika
1 oz (30g) nuts (any kind), ground
4 fl oz (120ml) thick natural yogurt
3 oz (85g) nuts (any kind), chopped
   fairly finely

American
1 teaspoonful paprika
¼ cupful nuts (any kind), ground
½ cupful thick plain yogurt
¾ cupful nuts (any kind), chopped
   fairly finely

1.   Stir paprika into the ground nuts.

2.   Add to the yogurt.

3.   Brown the chopped nuts under the grill.

4.   Mix into the yogurt.

5.   Serve as an hors d'oeuvre with crudités (thinly cut strips of raw
     vegetables) or as part of a salad.

NUT BUTTERS

Using an electric coffee mill grind any type of nuts into a soft powder.
Transfer them to a bowl and beat well until a butter is formed. A
little sea salt or finely minced herbs can be added. It is not necessary
to take off the skins.

Any nut can be made into a butter in this way. Brazils are the most
fatty and this butter is improved by the addition of a little lemon
juice. Almonds and cashews make a delicate butter. Minced parsley
or thyme go well with both of these.

BRAZIL FRUIT NOISETTES

Imperial (Metric)	American
4 oz (115g) cottage cheese	½ cupful cottage cheese
A little milk	A little milk
4 or 5 cubes pineapple (any fresh fruit can be used)	4 or 5 cubes pineapple (any fresh fruit can be used)
4 oz (115g) Brazil nuts, ground	¾ cupful Brazil nuts, ground
A little sea salt	A little sea salt
Sesame seeds or similar for coating	Sesame seeds or similar for coating

1. Beat cottage cheese to a smooth consistency with a little milk.

2. Chop pineapple well.

3. Mix all ingredients.

4. Form into balls and roll in sesame seeds.

5. Serve with salad or as an hors d'oeuvre on a bed of lettuce.

7.

PANCAKES, PASTA AND PIZZAS

PANCAKES

For pancakes it is better to use wholemeal flour with the bran sifted out in order to make sure that the final result is light. The mixture should be quite thin.

STANDARD PANCAKE BATTER

Imperial (Metric)	American
4 oz (115g) wholemeal flour	1 cupful wholewheat flour
1 tablespoonful sifted soya flour	1 tablespoonful sifted soya flour
Good pinch sea salt	Good pinch sea salt
1 large egg	1 large egg
½ pint (285ml) milk	1⅓ cupsful milk
Nut fat	Nut fat

1. Sieve the flours and salt together. Make a well in the centre and drop the egg and about half of the milk in it. Using a fork gradually whisk the flour into the centre mixture, adding more milk as you go along to obtain a thick creamy consistency. When all the milk is added the mixture should be smooth like *thin* cream.

2. Make the pancakes by first putting a little white nut fat in the pan, heating it and then pouring excess fat off into a basin. Stir the batter and pour enough to just cover the pan thinly. Cook on a moderate heat until the pancake can be shaken free — turn (toss if you can!) and cook the other side.

3. Keep hot on a plate over a pan of simmering water. Use for savoury or sweet dishes.

PASTA

If you have not eaten wholewheat pasta you have no idea what a real pasta dish is. There is no comparison between the insipid refined pasta which relies entirely on a sauce for taste and wholewheat pasta which has a truly delightful taste that complements the other ingredients in the dish.

Unfortunately the choice of shapes and sizes is limited, but improving all the time. Cooking times vary according to shape and size — but all pasta should be lowered gradually into boiling salted water into which about a teaspoonful of oil has been added. Stir occasionally to prevent sticking. Do not overcook — it should be *al dente*, that is, firm but not hard to the tooth.

LASAGNE LAYER

Imperial (Metric)	American
1 large onion, chopped	1 large onion, chopped
Oil for frying	Oil for frying
1 oz (30g) wholemeal flour	¼ cupful wholewheat flour
14 oz (395g) tin of tomatoes	Medium can of tomatoes
Good pinch of each of following: sea salt and freshly ground black pepper, garam masala, curry powder, oregano	Good pinch of each of following: sea salt and freshly ground black pepper, garam masala, curry powder, oregano
1 teaspoonful dry mustard	1 teaspoonful dry mustard
2 oz (55g) cheese, grated	½ cupful cheese, grated
½ lb (225g) wholewheat lasagne	8 ounces wholewheat lasagne

1. Fry the chopped onion in a little oil until it is transparent.

2. Stir in the flour and cook, stirring, for a few minutes. Add tomatoes, salt and pepper, a good pinch of garam masala, curry powder and oregano and the mustard. Stir well.

3. Simmer for 5 minutes.

4. Add the cheese, stir for 1 minute then take off heat, and keep warm.

5. Re-heat the lasagne carefully by shaking over heat in an oiled pan.

6. Check the tomato mixture for seasoning and adjust if necessary. Layer the lasagne and tomato mixture in a hot dish, finishing with a layer of the mixture.

7. Sprinkle with cheese and put under a moderate grill for a few minutes. The cheese can be omitted, in which case sprinkle with grated nuts.

MACARONI SALAD

Imperial (Metric)
½ lb (225g) wholewheat macaroni,
    cooked
6 oz (170g) peas, cooked
6 oz (170g) sweetcorn kernels,
    cooked
3 oz (85g) red or green pepper, raw,
    chopped
Mayonnaise (page 61)

American
8 ounces wholewheat macaroni,
    cooked
1 cupful peas, cooked
1 cupful sweetcorn kernels, cooked
½ cupful red or green pepper, raw,
    chopped
Mayonnaise (page 61)

1. Drain the cooked macaroni and refresh under cold water, drain
    well.

2. Mix it with peas, sweetcorn and pepper.

3. Toss in mayonnaise (page 61) to coat and serve with a lettuce,
    chicory or endive salad.

PASTA STEAMED SAVOURY

Imperial (Metric)
4 oz (115g) wholewheat spaghetti,
    cooked
½ pint (285ml) White Sauce (page
    64)
1 level teaspoonful dry mustard
1 tablespoonful tomato purée
4 oz (115g) Gouda or Edam cheese,
    grated
2 tomatoes, skinned and chopped
Sea salt and freshly ground black
    pepper

American
4 ounces wholewheat spaghetti,
    cooked
1⅓ cupsful White Sauce (page 64)
1 level teaspoonful dry mustard
1 tablespoonful tomato paste
1 cupful Gouda or Edam cheese,
    grated
2 tomatoes, skinned and chopped
Sea salt and freshly ground black
    pepper

1. Mix all ingredients gently together.

2. Pour them in to a greased container and cover with greased
    greaseproof paper and then aluminium foil.

3. To pressure cook — put about ½ pint/285ml (1⅓ cupsful) water with a squeeze of lemon juice in the cooker, stand the container on the trivet and bring to 15 pounds (6 kilos) pressure. Cook for 10 minutes and reduce at room temperature.

4. Serve with green vegetables, or on its own after a small salad.

SPAGHETTI WITH MUSHROOMS AND TOMATOES

Imperial (Metric)	American
½ lb (225g) wholewheat spaghetti	8 ounces wholewheat spaghetti
1 oz (30g) butter (or vegetable margarine)	2½ tablespoonsful butter (or vegetable margarine)
½ lb (225g) mushrooms, sliced	3 cupsful mushrooms, sliced
½ lb (225g) tomatoes, skinned and chopped	3 large tomatoes, skinned and chopped
Sea salt and freshly ground black pepper	Sea salt and freshly ground black pepper
Good pinch basil	Good pinch basil
Freshly grated nutmeg	Freshly grated nutmeg
2 tablespoonsful tomato purée	2 tablespoonsful tomato purée
2 or 3 tablespoonsful cream, top of milk or plant milk	2 or 3 tablespoonsful cream, top of milk or plant milk

1. Cook the spaghetti until *al dente*.

2. Meanwhile, melt butter in pan and add mushrooms, toss for a moment, then add tomatoes, sea salt and freshly ground black pepper, basil and nutmeg.

3. Shake together, and simmer with tight lid until mushrooms are tender.

4. Stir in the tomato purée, then add cream and stir for a moment.

5. Pour over the spaghetti on individual plates, or into a nest of pasta in a large dish. Sprinkle with parsley and serve.

PIZZAS

Pizzas make tasty and filling meals, but they are normally cooked in an oven. My recipes show you easy ways to make a pizza with nothing but one ring on which to cook.

You can use a frying pan, or the griddle. A topping can be prepared first and kept warm, or a simple topping of thin slices of tomato and cheeses will heat through as the second side cooks.

PAN-FRIED PIZZA

Imperial (Metric)	American
6 oz (175g) wholemeal flour	1½ cupsful wholewheat flour
Sea salt	Sea salt
1 teaspoonful baking powder	1 teaspoonful baking powder
A little water	A little water
Oil for frying	Oil for frying
Tomatoes, skinned and sliced thinly	Tomatoes, skinned and sliced thinly
Cheese, sliced thinly	Cheese, sliced thinly
Freshly ground black pepper	Freshly ground black pepper
Oregano or basil	Oregano or basil

1. Sift flour, salt and baking powder into a bowl, make a well in the centre and gradually add water working the flour into a dough.

2. Knead it until smooth, then roll out into one or two circles, depending on the size of your frying pan (or griddle). Make the circle quite thin.

3. Put onto a well greased pan over moderate heat. It should cook fairly slowly. When the underside is just browning turn over.

4. Carefully lay on tomatoes and cheese and sprinkle with black pepper and herbs. By the time the bottom is cooked the cheese should be nicely melted and tomatoes hot.

BREAD DOUGH PIZZA

Follow exactly the recipe for soft bread rolls on page 16. After first rising, shape into thin circles and place in an oiled plastic bag to rise again. When sufficiently risen follow recipe above for cooking.

TOPPINGS

Simple cheese and tomato toppings can be made more interesting by the addition of sliced olives, strips of pimento and capers, as well as circles of onion. These can all be added at the last stage since they do not need to be hot.

A more complicated topping needs to be made beforehand, and will be improved by a gentle 5 minutes under the grill.

MUSHROOM, EGG AND ONION TOPPING

Quantities depend on preference and size of pizzas

1. First hardboil the eggs, set them aside.

2. Sauté sliced onion with mushrooms in oil adding garlic if liked.

3. After a few moments add some sliced tomatoes with some sea salt and freshly ground black pepper, a grate of nutmeg, oregano and thyme.

4. Let it heat through — in fact cook just long enough to soften the mushrooms.

5. When pizza is ready slice the eggs and place on top, add the topping, sprinkle with grated cheese and put under the grill.

8.

RICE AND OTHER GRAINS

Whole rice and grains make a valuable addition to the diet. When cooked the rice will not look as white as polished rice, but the taste is not to be compared. It is the same for other grains: they do give a brownish look which may appear less than attractive to the uninitiated; but the taste is superior and food value far above devitalized processed food. Actually to the devotee of wholefoods the subtle colours of the various grains are much to be preferred to the dead whiteness of the processed varieties.

The recipes that follow are just a few ways in which rice and grains can form the main part of a meal. They are very satisfying and are generally best followed by a fruit sweet.

MILLET SAVOURY ROLY-POLY

For the pastry:

Imperial (Metric)	**American**
5 oz (140g) wholemeal flour	1¼ cupsful wholewheat flour
1 heaped tablespoonful flaked millet	1 heaped tablespoonful flaked millet
1 level tablespoonful soya flour	1 level tablespoonful soy flour
1 teaspoonful mixed herbs	1 teaspoonful mixed herbs
3 oz (85g) nut fat or white vegetable fat	⅓ cupful nut fat or white vegetable fat
1 teaspoonful yeast extract	1 teaspoonful yeast extract
Water to mix	Water to mix

For the filling:

Imperial (Metric)
1 onion, finely chopped
1 oz (30g) oil
2 sticks celery, chopped
1 small red pepper, chopped
2 tomatoes, skinned and chopped
1 chilli, chopped
1 tablespoonful tomato purée
Pinch of paprika, nutmeg and ginger
1/4 teaspoonful rosemary
Shake *Holbrooks* Worcester sauce
Water
4 oz (115g) millet flakes
2 oz (55g) Brazil nuts, finely ground
Sea salt and freshly ground black
  pepper

American
1 onion, finely chopped
2 tablespoonsful oil
2 stalks celery, chopped
1 small red pepper, chopped
2 tomatoes, skinned and chopped
1 chili, chopped
1 tablespoonful tomato paste
Pinch of paprika, nutmeg and ginger
1/4 teaspoonful rosemary
Shake vegetarian Worcester sauce
Water
1/2 cupful millet flakes
1/2 cupful Brazil nuts, finely ground
Sea salt and freshly ground black
  pepper

1. Make the pastry by stirring all dry ingredients together, then rub in fat with yeast extract and add enough water to make a stiff paste. Roll out into a square shape and set aside.

2. Make the filling by sautéing the onion in oil for a few minutes.

3. Then add celery, pepper, tomatoes, chilli, tomato purée, paprika, nutmeg and ginger, rosemary and Worcester sauce.

4. Mix all together and cook for a few minutes, add a little water then mix in millet and nuts, adding more water as necessary to make thick spreading consistency.

5. Cook for a few minutes, stirring. Taste and add sea salt and freshly ground black pepper if needed.

6. Cool a little then spread over pastry, leaving a little uncovered all round. Dampen edges, then carefully roll up.

7. Wrap in greaseproof paper and aluminium foil and steam for 1½ hours.

continued overleaf

Note: If using a pressure cooker, put the roly-poly on to the trivet when water is boiling in cooker, put on lid and allow to steam gently for 10 minutes, then put on 15 pounds (6 kilos) pressure and cook for 15 minutes, allow to reduce at room temperature.

MIXED GRAIN SAVOURY

Imperial (Metric)	American
2 oz (55g) each of brown rice, wheat, barley, rye	5 tablespoonsful each of brown rice, wheat, barley, rye
1 oz (30g) chick peas	2 tablespoonsful garbanzo beans
1 onion, chopped	1 onion, chopped
3 tablespoonsful olive oil (or similar)	3 tablespoonsful olive oil (or similar)
1 clove garlic, crushed	1 clove garlic, crushed
2 tablespoonsful tomato purée	2 tablespoonsful tomato paste
1 bay leaf	1 bay leaf
Sea salt and freshly ground black pepper	Sea salt and freshly ground black pepper
¾ pint (425ml) water	2 cupsful water
2 tomatoes, skinned and quartered	2 tomatoes, skinned and quartered

1. Soak the grains and chick peas (garbanzo beans) together overnight, then drain off water, and keep moist for 1 to 2 days.

2. Fry the onion over a gentle heat in a pan for about 5 minutes.

3. Add garlic, grains and chick peas (garbanzo beans), stir and cook for a further 5 minutes.

4. Add tomato purée, bay leaf and a little salt and pepper. Add water, bring to boil and simmer in a covered pan until all is cooked.

5. Taste and adjust seasoning, remove bay leaf, add tomatoes and gently stir. The grains should be separated. If there is any excess liquid drain it off and use for a sauce. Serve hot with green vegetables or cold with salad.

OATMEAL HODGILS

Imperial (Metric)	American
2 oz (55g) oatflakes or fine oatmeal	½ cupful oatflakes or fine oatmeal
½ oz (15g) nut fat	1¼ tablespoonsful nut fat
Sea salt	Sea salt
Chives, chopped	Chives, chopped

1. Season the oatmeal, add some chopped chives and then rub in the fat well.

2. Form into small balls, and pop into boiling soup for the last 20 minutes.

POTATO PIES

Use 1 good sized potato per person and enough Nut Savoury mixture (page 39) to fill each potato

1. Scrub potatoes clean, score with a fork, chop off top third, and a little from the bottom so it will stand up. Hollow out the centre (use this for soup).

2. Fill with the uncooked nut savoury and replace the top. Rub with oil and then wrap each potato in aluminium foil.

3. Steam in double steamer for about 1 hour — depending on the size of the potatoes. Alternatively use a pressure cooker. Put the potatoes on the trivet with enough water to cover trivet, bring to 15 pounds (6 kilos) pressure for 10-15 minutes — again depending on the size of the potatoes. Allow heat to reduce at room temperature.

Note: These potato pies are also good with the rice lentil mixture that follows — in which case it needs to be cooked before filling the potatoes.

You can use other fillings such as the *Sosmix* flattie mixture.

RICE LENTIL SQUARES

Imperial (Metric)	American
1 large onion, chopped	1 large onion, chopped
2 oz (55g) nut fat or white vegetable fat	¼ cupful nut fat or white vegetable fat
4 oz (115g) lentils	½ cupful lentils
6 oz (170g) brown rice, long-grain	¾ cupful brown rice, long-grain
1 clove garlic, crushed	1 clove garlic, crushed
Bay leaf	Bay leaf
Basil	Basil
Sea salt and freshly ground black pepper	Sea salt and freshly ground black pepper
4 tomatoes, skinned and chopped	4 tomatoes, skinned and chopped
1 tablespoonful wholemeal flour	1 tablespoonful wholewheat flour
Water	Water
Parsley, chopped	Parsley, chopped

1. Sauté the onion in fat for 5 minutes.

2. Add lentils and rice and shake to cover with fat.

3. Add garlic, a bay leaf, a little basil and seasoning with the tomatoes. Stir and cover with boiling water.

4. Cook with closed lid until soft.

5. Mix the flour with a little cold water, gradually add a little more water until it is a smooth cream.

6. Remove bay leaf when rice mixture is cooked, stir in flour mixture and cook for a few minutes, until the mixture is thick.

7. Transfer to a plate and allow to cool, then cut into squares and shallow fry them. Serve with green vegetables and a good sauce, sprinkled with chopped parsley.

SKIRLIE IN THE PAN

Imperial (Metric)	American
2 oz (55g) nut or vegetable fat	¼ cupful nut or vegetable fat
1 medium onion, finely chopped	1 medium onion, finely chopped
1 clove garlic, crushed (if liked)	1 clove garlic, crushed (if liked)
Medium oatmeal	Medium oatmeal
Sea salt and freshly ground black pepper	Sea salt and freshly ground black pepper

1. Heat fat in pan and then add the onions and garlic, and cook until they are transparent.

2. Add enough oatmeal, by degrees, to soak up all the fat, stir well until thoroughly cooked — it only takes a few minutes.

Note: This is surprisingly tasty, and goes with grated raw carrot and cabbage.

SPANISH WHEAT

Imperial (Metric)	American
½ lb (225g) whole wheat	1 cupful whole wheat
1 small onion, finely chopped	1 small onion, finely chopped
Oil for frying	Oil for frying
1 clove garlic, finely chopped	1 clove garlic, finely chopped
3 oz (85g) new peas	½ cupful new peas
1 small red pepper, diced	1 small red pepper, diced
Pinch of turmeric	Pinch of turmeric
Sea salt and freshly ground black pepper	Sea salt and freshly ground black pepper
Knob of vegetable margarine	Knob of vegetable margarine

1. First soak the wheat overnight and then leave moist for 1 or 2 days.

2. Fry onion in oil for a few minutes.

3. Add wheat and garlic and shake well, then cover with boiling water, stir and simmer with closed lid until wheat is cooked. This will be about 30 minutes, it should still be *al dente*.

4. Add peas, pepper, a pinch of turmeric, sea salt and freshly ground black pepper, stir and cook for 5 minutes (if peas are old they should be cooked before adding). Taste and season if needed, serve with knob of margarine on top. Good hot or cold with salad.

9.

SALADS AND SALAD DRESSINGS

Raw food is very necessary to the body; it retains maximum vitamins and supplies essential minerals as well as giving needed fibre to the digestive system.

To some people a 'salad' is a few pieces of lettuce, a tomato and some cooked beetroot laced with artificial dressing — eaten only in the summer time. This is a travesty of what a salad ought to be — which is, in essence, variety in texture and taste with raw foods predominating and dressings that enhance the food without swamping it.

If raw food is not already part of your daily diet you may like a few tips about making salads so attractive that they are irresistible to the most hardened 'anti-rabbit-food' eater.

1. Aim to steer reluctant salad eaters from the known to the unfamiliar: for example, start by introducing a little raw food among a lot of cooked.

2. Serve small portions at first.

3. Combine a small raw salad with some favourite food.

4. Be sure to serve with a dressing that is liked (even if it is bought 'artificial' — you can gradually change to something better).

5. To start the meal try making up a small salad in a bowl, top it with grated cheese and eat with a spoon.

6. If chewing is the problem start by grating everything with the finest grater.

Small Bowl Salad Suggestions

1. One heaped tablespoonful finely grated raw carrot. One heaped tablespoonful finely grated raw beetroot. A little chopped apple mixed with a few raisins, topped with a favourite dressing and with very thin sticks of celery popped into the top.

2. Two heaped tablespoonsful finely chopped raw cabbage, mixed with two chopped dates. Half a tomato sliced with dressing and a good sprinkling of finely grated cheese.

3. One heaped tablespoonful each finely chopped celery and apple on a bed of grated carrot, topped by one tablespoonful grated nuts with a round of pineapple. In the centre of the pineapple cottage or cream cheese spiked with chive stems or flowers.

Obviously ideas are endless — try any of the following (which is by no means an exhaustive list!):

Beetroot (beet), Brussels sprouts, carrot, parsnip, swedes (rutabaga), turnips — all raw, grated and mixed with lemon or orange juice or vinaigrette or mayonnaise.

Cabbage — red or white, finely chopped and mixed with raisins, chopped apple or orange segments, and with a light dressing.

Onion, leek — sliced in vinaigrette.

Avocado — sliced in vinaigrette or lemon juice.

Celery, chicory, chives, cucumber, endive, lettuce, mustard and cress, peppers, radishes, spring onions (scallions), tomatoes, watercress.

Dried and fresh fruit — occasionally tinned fruit.

Nuts and cheeses — grated.

Sproutings — give highest vitamins and taste value.

APPLE AND BEETROOT JELLY

Imperial (Metric)
1 pack commercial agar jelly, any flavour
2 apples, chopped
2 large beetroots, cooked and chopped
A few walnuts

American
1 pack commercial agar jello, any flavour
2 apples, chopped
2 large beets, cooked and chopped
A few walnuts

1. Make up jelly (jello) as instructions on packet.

2. Stir in chopped apple and beetroot (beet).

3. Pour into mould and leave to set.

4. Serve on a bed of lettuce sprinkled with walnuts.

Variation: To make a delicious Celery, Apple and Beet Jelly, grate the raw beetroot (beet), add 4 sticks of celery (chopped) and follow the recipe above for remaining ingredients and method.

SPROUTINGS

You can have the freshest, cheapest and easiest salad material growing on your own window sill all the year round by sprouting seeds and grains.

There are various kinds of specially manufactured 'sprouting farms', but an easy method is with a wide necked jar.

1. Cover the bottom of a clean glass jar with seeds, grains or beans.

2. Cover them with warm water.

3. Place this in a warm place (such as an airing cupboard) overnight. Have a porous cloth over the top of the jar.

4. In the morning drain off the water. Already the seeds will have become bigger!

5. For the next three to four days make sure that the seeds are always moist, but not wet. If they are kept in the dark and warm they will grow more quickly, but will also need more attention! If you keep them in front of you on the window sill you will not forget to put water in and drain it out once or twice a day.

Any whole seeds, grains and beans can be sprouted. Some are more tricky than others. For instance wheat needs to be fresh or it may not germinate well. Mung beans need more water.

If there is any sign of fermenting thoroughly rinse out the jar with water several times, and leave just moist, then the sproutings should be all right.

Use the sproutings after about 4 days when the vitamins are at their highest. The green shoot will be growing and reducing the vitamins, if you leave them any longer.

There are various recipes in this book using sproutings; they can be added to any salads, and are also good in soups. Throw them in just before you are ready to serve.

You can sprout most things, including alfalfa, chick peas, all sorts of beans, lentils, fenugreek, soya beans, wheat, oats, barley and rice.

MAYONNAISE

Imperial (Metric)	American
1 egg	1 egg
1 tablespoonful cider vinegar	1 tablespoonful cider vinegar
¼ teaspoonful sea salt	¼ teaspoonful sea salt
Freshly ground black pepper	Freshly ground black pepper
Pinch paprika and cayenne	Pinch paprika and cayenne
¼ teaspoonful dry mustard	¼ teaspoonful dry mustard
½ pint (285ml) olive oil	1⅓ cupsful olive oil
3 tablespoonsful lemon juice	3 tablespoonsful lemon juice
1 tablespoonful boiling water	1 tablespoonful boiling water

1. Put all ingredients, except the oil and lemon juice and water, into blender. Switch to top speed for 15 seconds, then stop. Remove lid, add a little oil, switch on and then off.

2. Do this several times to start blending in oil, then continue running machine while steadily adding oil.

3. When all oil is incorporated add 1 tablespoonful boiling water, switch on for 5 seconds then off, then add the lemon juice in the same way.

Note: This method should prevent curdling, but if the mayonnaise curdles, empty out goblet of all but a very little, add another whole egg. Mix, then gradually add the curdled mixture: it should come out perfectly.

VINAIGRETTE

Imperial (Metric)
1 part lemon juice or cider vinegar
2-3 parts oil (preferably olive oil)
Seasoning as above, with the
    addition of any chopped herbs

American
1 part lemon juice or cider vinegar
2-3 parts oil (preferably olive oil)
Seasoning as above, with the
    addition of any chopped herbs

1. Put all ingredients into a bottle or screw-top jar and shake vigorously. Garlic, if liked, can be added — just cut a piece of clove and keep whole in the bottle.

YOGURT DRESSING
A plain unsweetened yogurt makes a very good dressing thinned down with a little lemon or orange juice.

10.

SAUCES

A good sauce can lift a meal into the super class. It can also turn a few well-cooked vegetables into a satisfying meal. Here are some delicious sauces that could be used over vegetables or teamed with many of the savoury dishes given in this book.

REDCURRANT SAVOURY SAUCE

Imperial (Metric)
6 tablespoonsful redcurrant jelly
2 tablespoonsful cider vinegar

American
6 tablespoonsful redcurrant jelly
2 tablespoonsful cider vinegar

1. Melt jelly in a small pan over low heat.

2. Add vinegar, stirring, bring to boil and simmer for a minute or two to reduce and concentrate sauce.

BASIC WHITE SAUCE

Imperial (Metric)
¾ oz (20g) vegetable margarine
¾ oz (20g) wholemeal flour
½ pint (285ml) liquid, may be milk,
  or liquid from cooked vegetables

American
2 tablespoonsful vegetable
  margarine
2 tablespoonsful wholewheat flour
1⅓ cupsful liquid, may be milk, or
  liquid from cooked vegetables

1. Melt fat in saucepan then add flour, stir and cook for 1-2 minutes.

2. Remove pan from heat and gradually stir in half the liquid, beat smooth then add most of the remaining liquid. When sauce is smooth return to heat, bring slowly to boiling point stirring well all the time. Test for consistency and add the final drops of liquid if needed.

Variation: For **SORREL SAUCE** add to the above recipe a good handful fresh sorrel that has been chopped or put through herb mill with 5 or 6 spikes of chive, 2 sprigs lemon balm, add sea salt and freshly ground black pepper, and cook for a few minutes. Add 2 tablespoonsful white wine if desired.

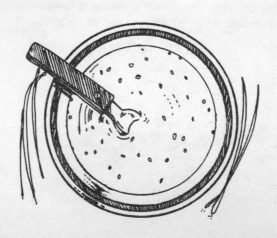

TOMATO WINE SAUCE

Imperial (Metric)
1 small onion, chopped
1 small carrot, chopped
1 tablespoonful oil
1 medium tin tomatoes
Sea salt and freshly ground black
  pepper
Tabasco
Basil
2 apricots, chopped
Pinch raw cane sugar
1 bay leaf
½ oz (15g) wholemeal flour
A little water
Red wine

American
1 small onion, chopped
1 small carrot, chopped
1 tablespoonful oil
1 medium can tomatoes
Sea salt and freshly ground black
  pepper
Tabasco
Basil
2 apricots, chopped
Pinch raw cane sugar
1 bay leaf
⅛ cupful wholewheat flour
A little water
Red wine

1. Sauté onion and carrot in oil.

2. Add tomatoes, seasoning, a shake of *Tabasco*, sprig basil (or pinch
    if dried), chopped apricots, sugar and bay leaf.

3. Simmer until all is soft then pass through a sieve.

4. Cream flour with a little water, add this to sauce, boil up, add
    wine to taste at this stage. Check seasoning and serve.

TANGY CHEESE SAUCE

Imperial (Metric)
1 oz (30g) vegetable margarine
1 oz (30g) wholemeal flour
½ pint (285ml) milk
1 small tart apple
4 oz (115g) Cheddar cheese, grated
Sea salt and freshly ground black
  pepper
Good pinch each of dry mustard and
  cayenne

American
2½ cupsful vegetable margarine
¼ cupful wholewheat flour
1⅓ cupsful milk
1 small sharp apple
1 cupful Cheddar cheese, grated
Sea salt and freshly ground black
  pepper
Good pinch each of dry mustard and
  cayenne

1. Make the sauce as described for Basic White Sauce (page 64).

2. Mix all other ingredients together then add them to sauce, mix well and cook for 3 minutes stirring.

3. Serve over vegetables or with fritters, rissoles etc.

11.

SOUPS

Soups are especially good preceding a salad meal. Vegetarian soups are tasty and nutritious, and not too time-consuming to make, particularly if a liquidizer is available. Bought vegetable bouillons help to improve flavour and a little soya flour beaten in gives creaminess and added goodness.

The following are a few suggestions from which other soups can be evolved.

ANY VEGETABLE SOUP

1. Clean and roughly chop about 5 different vegetables, such as onion, carrot, parsnip, swede (rutabaga) and celery, to make up to about 1 lb/455g (3 cupsful).

2. Put them in a pan with 1¾ pints/1 litre (4½ cupsful) stock or water. Add a sprinkling of brown rice, lentils or barley if you have it. Season, and add a vegetable bouillon or teaspoonful of yeast extract, and some herbs — such as thyme, mint and parsley, but try different ones.

3. Simmer until vegetables are all soft.

4. Liquidize them with a tablespoonful of soya flour. Return to heat, taste and adjust seasoning.

Note: If you do not have a liquidizer put the cooked vegetables through a *mouli*-sieve then add soya flour and reheat.

CREAM OF TOMATO SOUP

Imperial (Metric)	American
1 tablespoonful margarine, melted	1 tablespoonful margarine, melted
1 medium tin of tomatoes	1 medium can of tomatoes
1 onion, chopped	1 onion, chopped
1½ pints (850ml) water	3¾ cupsful water
Sea salt and freshly ground black pepper	Sea salt and freshly ground black pepper
2 cloves	2 cloves
1 bay leaf	1 bay leaf
1 tablespoonful soya flour	1 tablespoonful soy flour
1 teaspoonful raw cane sugar	1 teaspoonful raw cane sugar
Parsley, chopped	Parsley, chopped

1. Put margarine in pan and add vegetables, cook for a few minutes.

2. Add rest of ingredients except soya and parsley and sugar.

3. Simmer until soft.

4. Then either liquidize with soya, or pass through sieve and then add soya.

5. Return to pan, re-heat, add sugar, and taste and adjust. Serve with chopped parsley.

Note: To make soup with pressure cooker, put all ingredients except soya and parsley in cooker, bring to 15 pounds (6 kilos) pressure, simmer for 5 minutes and allow to reduce at room temperature, then continue as above.

WATERCRESS SOUP

Imperial (Metric)
1 oz (30g) vegetable margarine
1 small onion, chopped
1 potato, chopped
1 pint (570ml) vegetable stock, or
    milk and water
1 teaspoonful yeast extract
2 bunches of watercress, picked
    over and chopped
1 oz (30g) wholemeal flour
Seasoning
Grate of nutmeg

American
2½ tablespoonsful vegetable
    margarine
1 small onion, chopped
1 potato, chopped
2½ cupsful vegetable stock, or milk
    and water
1 teaspoonful yeast extract
2 bunches of watercress, picked
    over and chopped
¼ cupful wholewheat flour
Seasoning
Grate of nutmeg

1. Sauté the onion in fat for a few minutes.

2. Add the potato, liquid and yeast extract, simmer until vegetables are soft.

3. Put all ingredients into a liquidizer. Liquidize so that watercress is fairly small.

4. Return all to saucepan and cook, stirring just long enough to thicken. Taste and adjust. The soup will be a lovely green colour and very fresh tasting.

MAKE IT A MEAL SOUP

Imperial (Metric)

1 oz (30g) vegetable margarine
1 onion, chopped
2 potatoes, diced
1 large parsnip, thinly sliced
1 large carrot, in julienne (thin) strips
2 oz (55g) wholewheat macaroni rings
1 tablespoonful each of whole flaked barley, rye, wheat, lentils
A good handful of fresh herbs, such as sorrel, mint, thyme, marjoram, all chopped finely
2 tomatoes, skinned and chopped
1 tablespoonful tomato purée
1 teaspoonful yeast extract
Sea salt and freshly ground black pepper

American

2½ tablespoonsful vegetable margarine
1 onion, chopped
2 potatoes, diced
1 large parsnip, thinly sliced
1 large carrot, in julienne (thin) strips
½ cupful wholewheat macaroni rings
1 tablespoonful each of whole flaked barley, rye, wheat, lentils
A good handful of fresh herbs, such as sorrel, mint, thyme, marjoram, all chopped finely
2 tomatoes, skinned and chopped
1 tablespoonful tomato paste
1 teaspoonful yeast extract
Sea salt and freshly ground black pepper

In a slow-cooker:

1. Melt fat in a saucepan then add onion, cook for 2 minutes then add all root vegetables, shake to coat with fat.

2. Put slow-cooker on a low setting and add vegetables.

3. Boil 1½ pints/850ml (3¾ cupsful) water, add macaroni and cook for 5 minutes. Then add to the pot.

4. Stir in grains, lentils and herbs with chopped tomatoes, tomato purée and yeast extract.

5. Cook on low heat for 8 hours. Check 1 hour before serving for taste, season if needed. Also turn up to a high setting if vegetables are still uncooked.

In a pressure cooker:
1. Cook vegetables as above, then add water and all other ingredients except seasoning.

2. Bring to 15 pounds (6 kilos) pressure, simmer for 8 minutes, reduce at room temperature, taste, season and serve.

In a saucepan:
1. Proceed as for pressure cooker, but soup will need to simmer over a low heat for about 25 minutes.

Note: Serve this soup with bread rolls, cheese and apples to make a complete meal.

SPRING SOUP
In early springtime so-called weeds are fresh and can be used to make a good cheap soup.

1. Pick (with gloved hands) a good handful of stinging nettles, wash them over and chop and put into a pan.

2. Add the same of sorrel and chickweed, a few leaves of comfrey and some mint and thyme.

3. Chop an onion, carrot and potato and put them all together in the pan. Half fill with boiling water and simmer until all is cooked.

4. Put through *mouli*-sieve, return to pan, taste and add seasoning, some tomato purée and a little yeast extract if necessary.

Note: Quantities can be varied. The nettles of course lose their sting in cooking. They taste rather like spinach and can also be cooked and eaten as a vegetable.

12.

SOYA PROTEIN

The soya bean is used extensively as nutritious food. Soya can be bought as beans, flour or processed into various shapes that are sold dehydrated. When soaked these shapes take on the look and texture of meat — they come in mince and a variety of sizes of chunks. This soya protein is marketed by a number of firms under different trade names, and can be bought in packs of various sizes. Some wholefood shops sell bulk quantities at much reduced prices. In any case, a dish made with soya costs much less than a similar meat dish.

Soya protein can be unflavoured or with meaty flavours (the flavours are entirely non-animal in origin). The following recipes can be made with natural or flavoured varieties.

It should be noted that when hydrating natural soya protein a tasty liquid should be used, as soya absorbs the taste. Some people prefer to hydrate flavoured types with plain water. This can be done with all recipes; in which case be sure to deduct an appropriate amount of liquid. Hydrate the dried soya protein in about double its bulk of liquid.

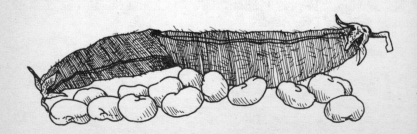

CURRY PANCAKES

Imperial (Metric)
1 onion, chopped
½ lb (225g) mushrooms, sliced
2 tablespoonsful oil
2 oranges
1 teaspoonful curry powder
¼ teaspoonful garam masala
¼ teaspoonful *Holbrooks* Worcester sauce
Sea salt and freshly ground black pepper
1 teaspoonful soya sauce
¼ pint (140ml) water
3 oz (85g) chunky tvp
Pancake batter (page 44)

American
1 onion, chopped
3 cupsful mushrooms, sliced
2 tablespoonsful oil
2 oranges
1 teaspoonful curry powder
¼ teaspoonful garam masala
¼ teaspoonful vegetarian Worcester sauce
Sea salt and freshly ground black pepper
1 teaspoonful soy sauce
⅔ cupful water
¾ cupful chunky tvp
Pancake batter (page 44)

1. Sauté onion and mushrooms in oil for a few minutes.

2. Squeeze half the orange and cut the other half into wedges.

3. Add orange juice, spices, sauces, seasoning and water to the pan.

4. Stir, bring gently to boil and simmer for 5 minutes, then add soya chunks.

5. Simmer for about 20 minutes until chunks are tender, stirring now and then.

6. While this is cooking make the pancakes (page 44) and keep warm on a hot plate over simmering water.

7. Test mixture for taste and adjust, then fill pancakes and serve with orange wedges.

GOULASH WITH SAUERKRAUT

Imperial (Metric)
5 oz (140g) chunky, flavoured tvp, hydrated in water, simmered 20 minutes
1 oz (30g) wholemeal flour
2 oz (55g) white nut fat (or vegetable fat)
2 tomatoes, skinned and quartered
1 green pepper, de-seeded and sliced
2 teaspoonsful paprika
Pinch of cayenne
½ lb (225g) sauerkraut
Seasoning
½ pint (285ml) sour cream

American
1¼ cupsful flavoured tvp, hydrated in water, simmered 20 minutes
¼ cupful wholewheat flour
¼ cupful white nut fat (or vegetable fat)
2 tomatoes, skinned and quartered
1 green pepper, de-seeded and sliced
2 teaspoonsful paprika
Pinch of cayenne
2 cupsful sauerkraut
Seasoning
1⅓ cupsful sour cream

1. Squeeze as much moisture from soya chunks as possible.

2. Roll them in the flour and sauté in fat in a saucepan. Toss until browned all over, remove with draining spoon and set aside.

3. Put tomatoes and pepper into saucepan with paprika and cayenne, stir and cook until soft.

4. Add sauerkraut and tvp chunks — bring to simmering point, taste and add seasoning if needed.

5. Just before serving add sour cream.

MEXICAN MINCE-UP

Imperial (Metric)	American
1 large onion, chopped	1 large onion, chopped
A little oil	A little oil
1 small tin tomatoes	1 small can tomatoes
1 medium tin red kidney (or soya) beans	1 medium can red kidney (or soy) beans
2 cloves garlic, finely chopped	2 cloves garlic, finely chopped
1 teaspoonful paprika	1 teaspoonful paprika
Pinch of cayenne	Pinch of cayenne
Shake of *Tabasco*	Shake of *Tabasco*
¼ pint (140ml) water	⅔ cupful water
Seasoning	Seasoning
4 oz (115g) tvp mince	½ cupful tvp mince

1. Sauté onion in oil until softened.

2. Add all other ingredients except soya mince.

3. Simmer for 5 minutes, then add mince.

4. Simmer for further 5 minutes when most of the liquid should be taken up. Serve hot with a chopped raw cabbage salad.

MINCE POTATO NEST

Imperial (Metric)
Oil for frying
1 onion, finely chopped
1 medium carrot, grated
1 small parsnip, grated
1 small piece turnip, grated
1 small tin tomatoes
1 clove garlic, crushed
1 teaspoonful yeast extract
1 teaspoonful dried or 3 or 4 leaves
  fresh basil, chopped
Sea salt and freshly ground black
  pepper
4 oz (115g) tvp mince
About 1½ lb (680g) potatoes,
  cooked and mashed with 1 oz
  (30g) vegetable margarine, 2 egg
  yolks, seasoning
2 tablespoonsful grated cheese

American
Oil for frying
1 onion, finely chopped
1 medium carrot, grated
1 small parsnip, grated
1 small piece turnip, grated
1 small can tomatoes
1 clove garlic, crushed
1 teaspoonful yeast extract
1 teaspoonful dried or 3 or 4 leaves
  fresh basil, chopped
Sea salt and freshly ground black
  pepper
1 cupful tvp mince
About 1½ pounds potatoes, cooked
  and mashed with 2½
  tablespoonsful vegetable
  margarine, 2 egg yolks, seasoning
2 tablespoonsful grated cheese

1. Put a little oil in a pan, add onion and root vegetables, cook for a moment, then add tomatoes, garlic, yeast extract, basil, sea salt and freshly ground black pepper.

2. Stir, add a little water to barely cover ingredients, then add soya mince. Cook for 5 minutes with tight lid.

3. Meanwhile pipe (or spread) hot potato mixture into a nest on a hot dish. (Reserve a little to pipe lattice on top.)

4. Test mince mixture and adjust taste, then pour it on to potato nest. Pipe lines over if wished and sprinkle with a little grated cheese.

5. Pop under grill to just melt cheese. (Cheese and egg yolks can be omitted if desired.)

QUICKER MINCE POTATO NEST

Imperial (Metric)	American
1 small tin condensed vegetable soup	1 small can condensed vegetable soup
4 oz (115g) tvp mince	1 cupful tvp mince
1 teaspoonful yeast extract	1 teaspoonful yeast extract
2 oz (55g) peas, cooked	1/3 cupful peas, cooked
1/4 pint (140ml) water	2/3 cupful water
1 teaspoonful dried or fresh basil	1 teaspoonful dried or fresh basil
Seasoning if needed	Seasoning if needed
About 1 1/2 lb (680g) potatoes, cooked and mashed with 1 oz (30g) vegetable margarine, 2 egg yolks, seasoning	About 1 1/2 pounds potatoes, cooked and mashed with 2 1/2 tablespoonsful vegetable margarine, 2 egg yolks, seasoning
2 tablespoonsful grated cheese	2 tablespoonsful grated cheese

1. Put the soup, soya mince, yeast extract, peas, water, basil and seasoning in a pan, stir well, bring to simmering point for 5 minutes.

2. Follow the recipe for Mince Potato Nest (page 76) from stage 3 onwards.

SOYA AND VEGETABLE STEW

Imperial (Metric)	American
3 large onions, chopped	3 large onions, chopped
1 carrot, sliced	1 carrot, sliced
1 raw beetroot, diced	1 raw beet, diced
2 tablespoonsful corn oil	2 tablespoonsful corn oil
1 medium tin tomatoes	1 medium can tomatoes
1 pint (570ml) vegetable stock or water	2½ cupsful vegetable stock or water
2 teaspoonsful tomato purée	2 teaspoonsful tomato paste
2 bay leaves	2 bay leaves
2 cloves garlic, crushed	2 cloves garlic, crushed
1 teaspoonful paprika	1 teaspoonful paprika
1 teaspoonful ground ginger	1 teaspoonful ground ginger
Pinch of cayenne	Pinch of cayenne
Grate of nutmeg	Grate of nutmeg
Seasoning	Seasoning
5 oz (140g) chunky tvp	1¼ cupsful chunky tvp

1. Fry the raw vegetables in oil for 5 minutes.

2. Add all ingredients except soya chunks. Simmer for 5 minutes.

3. Add chunks and simmer for 20 minutes.

4. Remove bay leaves, taste for flavour and adjust seasoning.

STEAMED SAVOURY PUDDING

Imperial (Metric)	American
1 onion, minced	1 onion, minced
1 tablespoonful oil	1 tablespoonful oil
1 tablespoonful tomato purée	1 tablespoonful tomato paste
¼ pint (140ml) water	⅔ cupful water
4 oz (115g) tvp mince	1 cupful tvp mince
½ lb (225g) wholemeal self-raising flour	2 cupsful wholewheat self-raising flour
Sea salt and freshly ground black pepper	Sea salt and freshly ground black pepper
2 oz (55g) wholemeal breadcrumbs	1 cupful wholewheat breadcrumbs
3 oz (85g) white vegetable fat	⅓ cupful white vegetable fat
1 tablespoonful parsley, minced	1 tablespoonful parsley, minced
Grated nutmeg	Grated nutmeg
¼ pint (140ml) milk or soya milk	⅔ cupful milk or soy milk

1. In a pan cook onion in oil until soft.

2. Add seasoning, tomato purée and water and mix, simmer for moment, then add mince and put aside.

3. Sieve flour with a little sea salt and freshly ground black pepper. Add breadcrumbs and rub in fat. Stir in rest of ingredients, add milk and mix well.

4. Grease a pudding basin, put in the mixture, cover with greased paper.

5. Have ready pressure cooker with trivet in place and water well covering trivet, add squeeze lemon juice. When water is boiling put in pudding, put on top of pressure cooker and gently steam for 15 minutes.

6. Bring to 15 pounds (6 kilos) pressure and cook for 30 minutes, reduce at room temperature.

Note: To steam without a pressure cooker the pudding needs 2 hours to cook.

TOMATO SOY SQUARES

Imperial (Metric)
1 oz (30g) white vegetable fat
1 medium onion, chopped finely
2 tomatoes, skinned and chopped
Bay leaf
Freshly ground black pepper
1 tablespoonful tomato purée
1 tablespoonful sesame salt
Pinch of mixed spices
Grated nutmeg
Good sprig of thyme
8 tablespoonsful water
4 oz (115g) soya flour
2 oz (55g) bran or wholemeal
  breadcrumbs
Sesame seeds or wholemeal
  breadcrumbs for coating
Oil for frying

American
2½ tablespoonsful white vegetable
  fat
1 medium onion, chopped finely
2 tomatoes, skinned and chopped
Bay leaf
Freshly ground black pepper
1 tablespoonful tomato paste
1 tablespoonful sesame salt
Pinch of mixed spices
Grated nutmeg
Good sprig of thyme
8 tablespoonsful water
1 cupful soy flour
1 cupful bran or wholewheat
  breadcrumbs
Sesame seeds or wholewheat
  breadcrumbs for coating
Oil for frying

1. Melt fat in saucepan, cook onion and tomatoes with bay leaf, black pepper, tomato purée, sesame salt, mixed spice, thyme and nutmeg for a few moments, then add water.

2. Simmer for 5 minutes.

3. Remove bay leaf and liquidize.

4. Return to saucepan and mix in soya flour and bran or breadcrumbs.

5. Spread mixture on a plate, cut into squares and leave to cool.

6. Dip in sesame seeds or breadcrumbs and shallow fry.

7. Once both sides are cooked, split down the middle and fry the uncooked side. This gives a thin crisp finish. Serve with a good tomato sauce and vegetables.

Note: The squares can be made without liquidizing, but may then take up less soya and bran.

STEAMED TOMATO SOY PUDDING

Recipe is exactly as above except that 2 eggs are beaten into the mixture after the soya flour is added. Then follow recipe for Steamed Savoury Pudding (page 79), but steam for 10 minutes followed by 25 minutes in pressure cooker, or 1½ hours in the ordinary way.

13.

SWEET DISHES

Many sweet dishes can be made without the use of the oven. The classic being fresh fruit salad for which a recipe is hardly needed. Suffice it to say that if fruit salad is made well in advance it is enhanced by the addition of a few sultanas and sometimes some tiger nuts. Jellies made with agar-agar can be used at half strength to hold the fruit together.

I have included a few rather unusual recipes which I hope will find a place in your repertoire.

CARAMELLED FRUIT

Imperial (Metric)
3 bananas, thickly sliced and
  sprinkled with lemon juice
2 oranges, segmented
4 oz (115g) stoned dates, chopped
  finely
2 oz (55g) tiger nuts, soaked
  overnight, drained
Natural yogurt
Raw cane sugar

American
3 bananas, thickly sliced and
  sprinkled with lemon juice
2 oranges, segmented
⅘ cupful stoned dates, chopped
  finely
¼ cupful tiger nuts, soaked
  overnight, drained
Plain yogurt
Raw cane sugar

1. Layer all fruit with tiger nuts in a nice flameproof dish.

2. Pour over yogurt to barely cover top layer.

3. Refrigerate for about 3 hours — or more.

4. Just before serving sprinkle with generous quantity brown sugar
   and put under grill for 3 minutes.

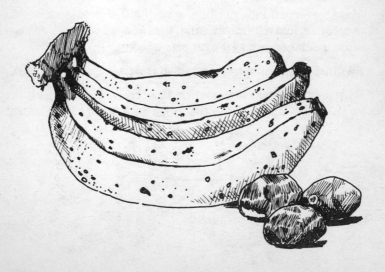

CHESTNUT SOUFFLÉ (COLD)

Imperial (Metric)	American
9 oz (255g) chestnut purée (unsweetened)	1 cupful chestnut paste (unsweetened)
2 oz (55g) raw cane sugar	⅔ cupful raw cane sugar
2 tablespoonsful brandy (optional)	2 tablespoonsful brandy (optional)
2 large eggs, separated	2 large eggs, separated
¼ pint (140ml) double cream	⅔ cupful heavy cream
½ pint (285ml) milk	1⅓ cupsful milk
2 level teaspoonsful agar-agar	2 level teaspoonsful agar-agar
½ cupful raspberries	½ cupful raspberries

1. First prepare a straight sided 6 inch (15cm) soufflé dish by tying a band of greaseproof paper round sides to stand 2 inches (5cm) above top.

2. Beat chestnut purée until it is soft then beat in sugar and brandy.

3. Whip egg whites and cream (separately) until stiff.

4. Dissolve agar-agar in a little milk then beat into rest of milk with the egg yolks. Stir this mixture in double saucepan over simmering water — continue stirring until mixture thickens (10-15 minutes).

5. Make sure cream and egg whites are still stiff. Reserve some cream to decorate, fold rest into mixture, then add egg whites. You need to be quick because agar-agar sets quickly.

6. Pile this with raspberries into dish (reserving a few for top).

7. Refrigerate for two hours, then pipe cream on top, with the raspberries. Can be kept in the fridge for a day or can be frozen.

FLAMBÉED BANANAS

Imperial (Metric)
2 oz (55g) butter
6 bananas, peeled and cut
   lengthways
1 apple, grated
3 oz (75g) raw cane sugar
Liqueur glass of rum or brandy

American
¼ cupful butter
6 bananas, peeled and cut
   lengthways
1 apple, grated
½ cupful raw cane sugar
Liqueur glass of rum or brandy

1. Melt butter in flameproof dish, cook bananas on both sides over moderate heat for 3-4 minutes.

2. Remove from heat, sprinkle with apple, then raw cane sugar. Warm the rum or brandy and flambé at table.

Variation: You can omit rum or brandy and grill sugared bananas for a few minutes before serving.

FRUIT UPSIDE-DOWN CAKE

Imperial (Metric)

2 oz (55g) vegetable margarine
4 oz (115g) vegetable margarine
4 oz (115g) raw cane sugar
2 level tablespoonsful honey
2 or 3 eggs
1 tablespoonful grated lemon peel
Small teaspoonful almond essence
Pinch sea salt, optional
10 oz (285g) wholemeal self-raising
   flour
¼ pint (140ml) milk and water
2 oz (55g) raw cane sugar
Any fresh fruit, sliced to cover
   bottom of pot

American

¼ cupful vegetable margarine
½ cupful vegetable margarine
⅔ cupful raw cane sugar
2 level tablespoonsful honey
2 or 3 eggs
1 tablespoonful grated lemon peel
Small teaspoonful almond essence
Pinch sea salt, optional
2½ cupsful wholewheat self-raising
   flour
⅔ cupful milk and water
⅓ cupful raw cane sugar
Any fresh fruit, sliced to cover
   bottom of pot

1. Melt 2 oz/55g (⅛ cupful) margarine in slow-cooker set at high.

2. Meanwhile make up cake mixture by the creaming method. Beat the margarine and sugar together with the honey. Add the eggs, one at a time, with the lemon peel, almond essence and pinch of sea salt (optional).

3. Gradually fold in the flour with the liquid to make a smooth consistency.

4. Brush sides of the slow-cooker with melted margarine then add the 2 oz/55g (⅓ cupful) sugar and spread over the base. Arrange fruit over the sugar then pour in cake mixture.

5. Cook at high setting for 1 hour then turn to low for 3½ hours or until cake is cooked. Turn out and serve hot or cold.

SWEET WHEAT

Imperial (Metric)
4 oz (115g) soft whole wheat grains
1 oz (30g) raw cane sugar
2 tablespoonsful brandy, rum or
    apricot juice
Water

American
½ cupful soft whole wheat grains
2 tablespoonsful raw cane sugar
2 tablespoonsful brandy, rum or
    apricot juice
Water

1. Proceed as for sprouting wheat (page 60) for two days, making sure wheat is not left soaking after first 12 hours, but is kept moist.

2. When wheat has swollen and is just beginning to sprout put it in a pressure cooker, just cover with water, bring to 15 pounds (6 kilos) pressure for 10 minutes, reduce at room temperature.

3. Drain off any excess water, add sugar and rum, brandy or juice. Serve hot, or refrigerate for several hours before serving.

LEMON CHEESECAKE

For flan case:

Imperial (Metric)	American
3 oz (85g) vegetable margarine	⅓ cupful vegetable margarine
8 oz (225g) digestive biscuits	1 cupful Graham crackers
1 heaped tablespoonful molasses or honey	1 heaped tablespoonful molasses or honey
A little grated lemon rind	A little grated lemon rind
1 teaspoonful cinnamon	1 teaspoonful cinnamon
Grate of nutmeg	Grate of nutmeg

For filling:

Imperial (Metric)	American
3 oz raw cane sugar	3 oz raw cane sugar
1½ oz (45g) vegetable margarine	3¾ tablespoonsful vegetable margarine
1 teaspoonful cinnamon	1 teaspoonful cinnamon
1 egg yolk	1 egg yolk
5 tablespoonsful double cream	5 tablespoonsful heavy cream
6 oz (170g) cream cheese (cottage cheese can be used)	¾ cupful cream cheese (cottage cheese can be used)
1 tablespoonful lemon juice	1 tablespoonful lemon juice

1. Grease a 7 inch (18cm) flan tin.

2. Melt margarine in saucepan, mix in all other ingredients for flan case.

3. Pour into loose-based flan tin, pressing down well and flattening the top.

4. Put into refrigerator for several hours to set — or deep freeze for 1 hour. Then turn out onto flat dish.

5. Cream butter and sugar with cinnamon, beat in yolk and the cream, then beat in cheese and lemon juice.

6. Fill flan, fork top decoratively then put in fridge or deep freeze. Before serving top can be piped with more cream or decorated with a few nibbed almonds etc.

PINK RICE DELIGHT

Imperial (Metric)
1 oz (30g) vegetable margarine
2 oz (55g) sweet or short-grain brown rice*
1 pint (570ml) milk
4 or 5 glacé cherries
1 tablespoonful mixed dried fruit
1 tablespoonful whole almonds

American
2½ tablespoonsful vegetable margarine
¼ cupful sweet or short-grain brown rice*
2½ cupsful milk
4 or 5 glacé cherries
1 tablespoonful mixed dried fruit
1 tablespoonful whole almonds

1. Melt margarine in pressure cooker, add rice and shake for a moment. Add all other ingredients, bring to simmer.

2. Put on lid and bring to 15 pounds (6 kilos) pressure gradually.

3. Cook for 10 minutes, reduce heat at room temperature.

*If ordinary short-grain brown rice is used a little raw cane sugar may be needed.

Note: This is delicious hot or cold with vanilla ice cream. Non-animal milks can be used to make this sweet.

RASPBERRY AND RECURRANT PURÉE

Imperial (Metric)
Equal quantities raspberries and
  redcurrants
Water to cover
Sugar to taste
Wholemeal flour (if bran is sieved
  out the appearance will be better)

American
Equal quantities raspberries and
  redcurrants
Water to cover
Sugar to taste
Wholemeal flour (if bran is sieved
  out the appearance will be better)

1. Simmer fruit with enough water to cover until fruit is absolutely soft.

2. Sieve and return to rinsed saucepan, add a little sugar to taste (better if not too sweet).

3. Add 1 teaspoonful wholemeal flour to each ½ pint/285ml (1⅓ cupsful) purée. Stir well, bring to boil. Then pour into dish. This will not be completely set. Keeps in fridge for several days.

Note: Gives extra 'something' to both Chestnut Soufflé (page 84) and Sweet Wheat (page 87).

14.

VEGETABLES

Vegetarian cooking makes more imaginative use of vegetables. When cooking any kind of vegetable it is essential to retain as much of the goodness as possible, and so they should be cooked in very little water or, better still, steamed.

The recipes in this section use mostly everyday vegetables, and the secret of their success is in the addition of spices, herbs and flavourings.

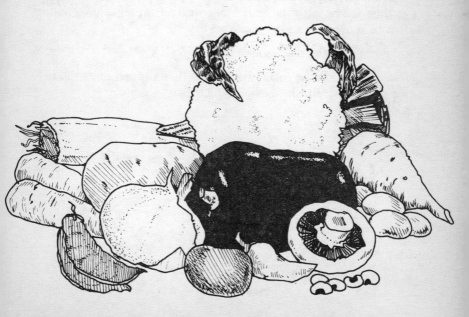

BEAN FLATTIES

Imperial (Metric)

9 oz (225g) kidney, soya or butter beans (this is drained weight cooked — they can be tinned or soaked and cooked yourself)

2 oz (55g) bran

1 oz (30g) white vegetable fat, grated

1 onion, grated

1 tablespoonful tomato purée

1 tablespoonful dried or fresh chopped winter savory (or use rosemary)

Sea salt and freshly ground black pepper

American

1½ cupsful kidney, soy or Lima beans (this is drained weight cooked — they can be canned or soaked and cooked yourself)

½ cupful bran

2½ tablespoons white vegetable fat, grated

1 onion, grated

1 tablespoonful tomato paste

1 tablespoonful dried or fresh chopped winter savory (or use rosemary)

Sea salt and freshly ground black pepper

1. Mash the beans, then mix them with all other ingredients. Alternatively, beans, onion and fat can be put through a mincer then mixed with the rest. Make into a firm texture by adding a little more bran if necessary.

2. Form into flat shapes and shallow fry.

Note: Flatties can be coated in egg and then dipped in oatflakes to give nicer crisp finish.

BUTTER BEAN BURGERS

Imperial (Metric)	American
½ lb (225g) butter beans, cooked	1⅓ cupsful Lima beans, cooked
2 oz (55g) vegetable margarine	¼ cupful vegetable margarine
2 tablespoonsful tomato ketchup	2 tablespoonsful tomato catsup
Shake *Tabasco*	Shake *Tabasco*
Sea salt and freshly ground black pepper	Sea salt and freshly ground black pepper
Sesame seeds or flaked oatmeal	Sesame seeds or flaked oatmeal

1. Mash butter (Lima) beans, then beat in margarine and rest of ingredients except sesame seeds or oatmeal.

2. Form mixture into round shapes and dip in seeds or oatmeal. Shallow fry.

Note: Butter (Lima) beans are always improved if they are cooked with a sprig of winter savory.

CHIVE POTATO CAKES

Imperial (Metric)	American
About 1 lb (455g) potatoes, cleaned, unpeeled and coarsely grated	About 1 pound potatoes, cleaned, unpeeled and coarsely grated
Handful chives, chopped finely	Handful chives, chopped finely
Handful sprouted fenugreek (or other seed, such as alfafa)	Handful sprouted fenugreek (or other seed, such as alfafa)
1 oz (30g) soya flour	¼ cupful soy flour
Sea salt and freshly ground black pepper	Sea salt and freshly ground black pepper
1 oz (30g) white vegetable fat	2½ tablespoonsful white vegetable fat

1. Squeeze out as much moisture as possible from the potatoes.

2. Mix in all other ingredients except fat.

3. Heat fat in a pan. Place spoonfuls of the mixture in pan, neaten them and cook for about 5 minutes, then turn to cook other side.

4. Chive Potato Cakes can be sprinkled with grated cheese towards end of cooking.

CRISPY POTATOES

Without an oven one cannot have roast potatoes, but this way gives a crisp finish.

1. Cut the potatoes into quarters and boil in as little salted water as possible (or steam) until potatoes are about half cooked.

2. Drain and dry then transfer to frying pan and finish cooking in a little oil or white vegetable fat on a medium heat, turning to brown all sides.

DROP VEGETABLE PANCAKES

Imperial (Metric)	American
1 small onion	1 small onion
1 medium carrot	1 medium carrot
1 large potato	1 large potato
1 piece swede	1 piece rutabaga
2 sticks celery	2 stalks celery
Handful of spinach	Handful of spinach
Sea salt and freshly ground black pepper	Sea salt and freshly ground black pepper
Bouquet garni	Bouquet garni
1 egg	1 egg
2 tablespoonsful soya flour	2 tablespoonsful soy flour
Grated nutmeg	Grated nutmeg
Soya sauce	Soy sauce
Ground nuts, any variety	Ground nuts, any variety
Oil for frying	Oil for frying

1. Chop and cook all vegetables in a little water with seasoning and *bouquet garni* until just soft.

2. Pass through *mouli*-sieve, add egg, soya flour, nutmeg and soya sauce.

3. Return to saucepan and heat to thicken, taste and add seasoning, ground nuts. Stir well.

4. Drop in spoonsful on to hot shallow fat in frying pan. Turn when cooked on one side.

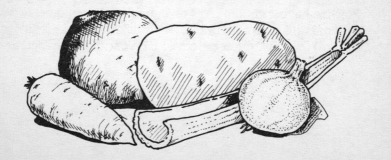

LEEKS IN A NEST

Imperial (Metric)	American
2 large leeks, washed and cut into rings	2 large leeks, washed and cut into rings
1 medium onion, chopped	1 medium onion, chopped
3 tablespoonsful oil	3 tablespoonsful oil
2 oz (55g) button mushrooms	1 cupful button mushrooms
Sea salt and freshly ground black pepper	Sea salt and freshly ground black pepper
Pinch of cayenne	Pinch of cayenne
Grate of nutmeg	Grate of nutmeg
1 clove garlic, crushed	1 clove garlic, crushed
2 oz (55g) wholewheat macaroni rings, cooked	½ cupful wholewheat macaroni rings, cooked
3 tomatoes, skinned and quartered	3 tomatoes, skinned and quartered
About 1 lb (455g) potatoes, cooked and mashed	About 1 pound potatoes, cooked and mashed
½ a lemon, cut in wedges	½ a lemon, cut in wedges
A few black olives	A few black olives

1. Sauté leeks and onion in oil for a few minutes.

2. Add whole mushroom cups and chopped stalks, season with salt and pepper, add pinch of cayenne, grate nutmeg and the garlic.

3. Shake together, put on lid and cook for 5-8 minutes, shaking now and then to avoid burning, and keep food whole.

4. Test to see if cooked, then add macaroni rings, stir in then add tomatoes, keep on heat just long enough to heat all through.

5. Pipe the hot potato into nests on individual dishes, quickly fill with mixture. Top with one or two black olives and put under the grill for a few minutes to heat. Serve with lemon wedges.

LEEK AND EGG SPECIAL

Imperial (Metric)	American
2 leeks, well washed and cut into 1 inch (2cm) lengths	2 leeks, well washed and cut into 1 inch lengths
A little oil for frying	A little oil for frying
3 large eggs	3 large eggs
¼ pint (140ml) milk	⅔ cupful milk
4 tablespoonsful cream or top of milk	4 tablespoonsful cream or top of milk
Sea salt and freshly ground black pepper	Sea salt and freshly ground black pepper
½ pint (285ml) thick Tomato Wine Sauce (page 65)	1⅓ cupsful thick Tomato Wine Sauce (page 65)
2 tablespoonsful Parmesan cheese	2 tablespoonsful Parmesan cheese
2 tablespoonsful wholemeal breadcrumbs	2 tablespoonsful wholewheat breadcrumbs

1. Cook leeks in boiling salted water for 5 minutes.

2. Drain and dry well on kitchen paper. Put them into oiled frying pan. Mix eggs with milk, cream and seasoning, then pour over leeks. Gently cook over medium heat. Heat up the Tomato Wine Sauce.

3. When egg mixture is cooked remove to serving dish, pour the sauce over, sprinkle with a mixture of Parmesan and wholemeal breadcrumbs.

4. Heat under moderate grill. Serve with baked beans and potatoes.

STUFFED CABBAGE WITH ORANGE

Imperial (Metric)
12 cabbage leaves
1 onion, chopped
4 oz (115g) Brazil or hazelnuts,
  ground
2 oz (55g) bran
2 oz (55g) rye flakes (or wheat)
2 oz (55g) sprouted chick peas
2 oz (55g) soya flour
Several sprigs fresh thyme, chopped
Sea salt and freshly ground black
  pepper
Water or vegetable stock
1 orange, sliced
Juice of 2 oranges
Medium tin of tomatoes

American
12 cabbage leaves
1 onion, chopped
1 cupful Brazil or hazelnuts, ground
½ cupful bran
1¼ cupsful rye flakes (or wheat)
1 cupful sprouted garbanzo beans
½ cupful soy flour
Several sprigs fresh thyme, chopped
Sea salt and freshly ground black
  pepper
Water or vegetable stock
1 orange, sliced
Juice of 2 oranges
Medium can of tomatoes

In a slow-cooker:

1. Immerse cabbage leaves in boiling water for 1 minute, refresh in cold water and drain.

2. Put aside orange, orange juice and tomatoes, mix all other ingredients adding just enough water or stock to make a firm consistency. Do not over season as flavours are increased by the use of a slow-cooker.

3. Stuff cabbage leaves by putting some filling at the stalk end (cutting 'v' in stalk to facilitate folding) then rolling up and tucking sides under.

4. Place the stuffed cabbage leaves in slow-cooker.

5. Mix orange juice with tomato juice from the tin, chop tomatoes and pour all over the leaves.

6. Cook on low heat for 6-8 hours or 3-4 hours on high heat. Serve garnished with orange slices.

RUNNER BEAN SPECIAL

Imperial (Metric)	American
1 small onion, chopped	1 small onion, chopped
Oil for frying	Oil for frying
1 tomato, chopped	1 tomato, chopped
Soya sauce	Soy sauce
A few drops chilli sauce	A few drops chili sauce
2 tablespoonsful cashew nuts, chopped	2 tablespoonsful cashew nuts, chopped
About 1 lb (455g) fresh runner beans, cooked	About 1 pound fresh green beans, cooked

1. Fry onion in oil until just softened. A wok would be best for this recipe, but a frying pan could be used.

2. Add tomato and cook for 1 minute, then add a good shake of soya sauce and the chilli sauce. Mix gently and cook for further 1 minute.

3. Brown cashews under the grill.

4. Stir onion mix gently into hot beans and serve sprinkled with cashews.

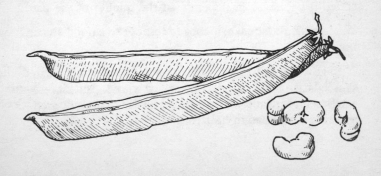

STUFFED MARROW

Imperial (Metric)	American
1 young medium-sized marrow	1 young medium-sized squash
A little oil or white nut fat	A little oil or white nut fat
Finely diced carrot and onion, enough to cover base of saucepan	Finely diced carrot and onion, enough to cover base of saucepan
Water if needed	Water if needed

For the stuffing:

Imperial (Metric)	American
2 oz (55g) cashew nuts, ground	½ cupful cashew nuts, ground
1 oz (30g) soya flour	¼ cupful soy flour
Handful of sprouted wheat	Handful of sprouted wheat
1 oz (30g) flaked barley or rye	½ cupful flaked barley or rye
3 or 4 dried apricots, finely chopped	3 or 4 dried apricots, finely chopped
Holbrooks Worcester sauce	Vegetarian Worcester sauce
Sea salt and freshly ground black pepper	Sea salt and freshly ground black pepper

1. Wipe marrow (squash), cut it in thick slices, scoop out centres and put them in a bowl to add to stuffing.

2. Sauté the diced carrot and onion in a saucepan for a few minutes. Lay marrow (squash) rings on top. Cover with lid, cook for 5 minutes, shaking now and then to avoid burning. It should be possible to cook without adding water, but a little water can be added if necessary (it depends on the quality of the pan).

3. When marrow (squash) is cooked remove to a hot dish and keep hot.

4. If marrow (squash) seeds are young and tender add them to the sautéed carrot and onion, chopped or whole. Add all remaining stuffing ingredients, stir and moisten with water if needed. Cook for 2 or 3 minutes to heat through.

5. Taste and adjust seasoning, fill marrow (squash) rings — set under grill to make sure it is hot. Serve with a good sauce and Crispy Potatoes (page 94).

SWEET AND SOUR CHINESE LEAVES

Imperial (Metric)	American
Oil for frying	Oil for frying
1 onion, cut in rings	1 onion, cut in rings
2 tablespoonsful Muscovado sugar	2 tablespoonsful Muscovado sugar
Juice of 1 lemon	Juice of 1 lemon
2 tablespoonsful cider vinegar	2 tablespoonsful cider vinegar
1 tablespoonful tomato purée	1 tablespoonful tomato paste
2 teaspoonsful soya sauce	2 teaspoonsful soy sauce
Sea salt and freshly ground black pepper	Sea salt and freshly ground black pepper
Shake of *Tabasco*	Shake of *Tabasco*
½ head Chinese leaves, shredded finely	½ head Chinese leaves, shredded finely

1. Heat the oil in centre of wok or frying pan, add onion rings and stir-fry.

2. When the onion has softened, add all the ingredients, keeping the Chinese leaves until last, and making sure that all the ingredients are well blended before leaves are added.

3. Stir in the leaves, mix well and cover the pan for about 5 minutes stirring frequently. The leaves should not go soggy.

Note: The best way to stir-fry is to use a wok, as its inverted dome shape facilitates light cooking of vegetables. However, a large frying pan (skillet) can be used.

SPINACH WITH ALMONDS

Imperial (Metric)
About 1 lb (455g) fresh spinach
1 tablespoonful vegetable margarine
2 tablespoonsful onion, chopped
Sea salt and freshly ground black
  pepper
2 tablespoonsful almonds,
  unskinned, chopped

American
About 1 pound fresh spinach
1 tablespoonful vegetable margarine
2 tablespoonsful onion, chopped
Sea salt and freshly ground black
  pepper
2 tablespoonsful almonds,
  unskinned, chopped

1. Lightly cook the spinach without water — shaking now and then to avoid burning. Drain liquid and keep for use in a soup or sauce.

2. Lightly chop spinach and mix with vegetable margarine and onion. Season.

3. Brown almonds under grill and sprinkle over before serving.

15.

WHOLE MENUS WITHOUT USING AN OVEN

Preparing interesting meals without the use of an oven really presents one basic problem — that of keeping food hot while the rest is still cooking.

If you have three or four rings the problem is not so great, since you can arrange for the various sections of the meal to be ready at more or less the same time — or you can keep food hot by placing it on top of a pan of simmering water over a spare ring. A grill is a great help in re-heating food for serving.

If you are limited to one or even two rings you must plan carefully. Good use can be made of wide-necked vacuum flasks. They will not only keep soups and sauces hot for many hours, but can be used to finish the cooking process of vegetables. A large food muff is also ideal for keeping food in pans hot (see page 12).

With a pressure cooker you can cook several vegetables at the same time, and the last of the cooking process can be done off the heat — thus releasing the ring for the rest of the meal.

Various electric saucepans, frying pans and slow-cookers are a great help where cooking facilities are limited, but of course they are expensive.

The bamboo steaming rings mentioned on page 9 are cheap and would be particularly useful on a boat, caravan or out of doors — as well as in a bed-sit!

The following complete menus give some ideas about planning quite complicated meals. The first four assume the use of only one ring, with no extra electrical equipment and no grill; 5 to 7 assume one ring with a grill; and 8 to 10 are planned for at least two rings with a grill available.

MENU 1

Cream of Tomato Soup (page 68)
Cheese Aigrettes (page 20) with boiled potatoes and green peas
Fresh fruit

Make the soup first and put into a wide necked flask. Boil potatoes with peas in steamer on top. When they are not quite cooked, drain potatoes (you could add liquid to soup) put a knob of butter in potatoes and peas and then put them aside — in food muff or wrapped up.

Make aigrettes while potatoes are cooking. Fry them quickly, as they are ready put on heated plate either over peas or wrapped in foil.

As last of aigrettes are cooking, serve soup.

MENU 2

Small bowl salad no 2 (page 58)
Pasta Steamed Savoury (page 46)
Raspberry and Redcurrant Purée with cream (page 90)

Make the sweet the day before and keep in fridge or cool place. Pasta and sauce can be prepared well in advance.

Salad is prepared while pasta dish is cooking. When cooker is de-pressurized take off lid and put serving dish and plates on top to heat while salad is being eaten.

MENU 3

Watercress Soup (page 69)
Stir-fried Vegetable with Eggs, and brown rice (page 32)
Lemon Cheesecake (page 88)

Lemon Cheesecake can be made the day before and kept in fridge.

Prepare the soup and put into wide necked vacuum flask. While you are cutting up vegetables cook the rice — set it aside in food muff or wrapped up in cloth about 5 minutes before it is actually cooked, or it can be put into another wide necked vacuum flask, in which case it need only be cooked for 5 minutes and finished off in flask.

MENU 4

Any Vegetable Soup (page 67)
Almond Prune Noisettes (page 35) on apple rings
Salad: grated raw carrot and beetroot (beet) (page 58) with yogurt
    dressing. Raw cabbage chopped mixed with sunflower seeds and sprouted
    wheat
Sliced tomatoes with onion rings in Vinaigrette (page 62)
Soft Wholemeal Bread Rolls (page 16)
Pink Rice Delight (page 89)

Make soup and set aside in vacuum flask.

Cook the Pink Rice Delight and set it aside — either allowing to cool or keep hot in pressure cooker or food muff.

If you want to have the bread rolls hot, make the dough so it is ready to cook just before the meal. You can prepare the salad while the rolls are cooking.

It is a good idea to slice onion rings and marinate them in the vinaigrette for several hours before they are needed.

MENU 5

Small bowl salad no 1 (page 58)
Broccoli Cheese (page 19) with boiled potatoes
Caramelled Fruit (page 83)

Make the sweet well beforehand and refrigerate. Make Tangy Cheese Sauce and keep hot in vacuum flask. While broccoli is cooking in steamer over potatoes make the salad.

Serve salad while broccoli is under low grill.

Take the sweet from the fridge some time in advance and sprinkle with sugar — allow to stand (so dish is not too cold to go under grill). Pop under grill while *entrée* dishes are being cleared away.

MENU 6

Lasagne Layer Savoury (page 45) with a side salad of grated raw carrot
     and parsnip on a bed of chicory or endive with onion rings in vinaigrette
     (page 62)
Fresh fruit salad and jelly

Prepare fruit salad and jelly and put into cool place or fridge. Cook
lasagne and put aside. Onion rings can be prepared in advance and
marinated in vinaigrette.

Prepare rest of salad while lasagne is cooking.

Make tomato mixture — then keep it hot in pan while you re-heat
lasagne.

Heat serving dish by rinsing with hot water or putting under *very*
low grill for a few minutes.

Make up savoury and put under grill — set out salad with onion
rings and serve with lasagne.

MENU 7

Parsnip Soup (page 67)
Brazil Nut Croquettes (page 36)
Large raw salad
Fruit Filled Drop scones (page 14) with cream

Make soup, using Any Vegetable Soup (page 67) recipe but omit
carrots and celery, only use small amount onion and swede (rutabaga)
with extra parsnips. Keep hot in vacuum flask.

Prepare nut croquettes mixture — shape and set ready to cook.
Prepare salad.

Drop Scones can be made well in advance.

To serve croquettes hot, cook them just before serving, leave in
frying pan on *very* low heat while serving soup. While main course
is being eaten have Drop Scones on a plate over simmering water
in saucepan.

Split Drop Scones, fill with raspberries or strawberries, replace
tops, sprinkle with Muscovado sugar and put under grill for 2 minutes.

MENU 8

Small salad of selection raw vegetables grated with a little cheese and
  mayonnaise
Rice Lentil Square (page 54) with
Tomato Wine Sauce (page 65), Brussels sprouts and potatoes
Fresh fruit salad

First make the sauce and put in vacuum flask to keep hot. Then cook
lentil with rice mixture. After 8 minutes put potatoes on to cook with
sprouts added in steamer after another 10 minutes.

Have squares ready to fry soon after potatoes are put on to cook.
Fruit salad can be made well in advance.

Small salad can be prepared while rice/lentil mixture is cooking.

MENU 9

Small bowl salad of grated raw carrot, beetroot (beet), Brussels sprouts and
  cabbage all mixed together with raisins and a few olives and mayonnaise
Mince Potato Nest (page 76)
Fruit Pancake (page 44) with sliced banana and dates moistened with a
  little lemon juice or rum

Have salad ready first, start the potatoes cooking, then make pancakes,
keeping them hot on a plate over potatoes. Start mince 5 minutes
before potatoes are ready (transfer pancakes over to the mince saucepan
and then over simmering water). Mash potatoes, finish dish and put
under grill.

Prepare pancake filling and fill and roll up pancakes. Serve salad.
When you remove Mince Potato Nest from grill sprinkle Muscovado
sugar on pancakes and put under very low grill.

MENU 10

Spring Soup (page 71)
Stuffed Tomatoes (page 29) with peas and chopped potatoes
Sweet Wheat (page 87)

Prepare soup and put into vacuum flask to keep hot. Use one ring to cook sweet wheat.

Partly cook potatoes with peas on steaming ring for about 8 minutes, during which time you can prepare the tomatoes. Take potatoes off ring, drain (using liquid either to add to soup or for stuffing mixture). Put peas in another vacuum flask to finish cooking. Cook stuffing mixture and put in tomatoes, put them under gentle grill. Then fry sliced potatoes in oil. Serve soup while potatoes are finishing cooking.

16.

MICROWAVE COOKERY

Since this book was first published microwave ovens have become more common in the home. I find mine enormously useful, for heating up food, thawing from the freezer and of course as a cooker in its own right. So I am pleased to have the opportunity to add a chapter about microwave cooking with vegetarian wholefood recipes to this collection.

Microwave ovens have been proved to be safe as long as they are kept air-tight — which basically means not banging the door shut or damaging it in any way.

Hints About Choosing a Microwave Oven

There is plenty of literature now about these ovens, and it is wise to read as much as possible. My advice would be to choose one with a turntable . . . without this you need to stop the oven and turn once or twice during cooking. All my recipes assume that there is a turntable in your oven. Be sure to have a variable heat: this makes it possible to cook foods that might otherwise spill over. The food is brought up to boiling point and then subsides before overflowing, provided the dish is not too full. I also find that bread is better if cooked for slightly longer on the variable setting. If you have a freezer, or ever buy frozen food you will also need to be able to defrost in your microwave, this setting thaws without cooking.

Apart from making sure that you are able to put a good sized dish into the oven you should remember that microwaves act differently from normal oven heat. In practice this means the larger amount of food the longer time is needed to cook. As food stays hot for a long time when taken out of the microwave oven (indeed continues to cook in some cases) it is often better to put smaller amounts in at a time rather than crowding (as one might do with a conventional oven in order to make full use of the heat).

Even if you are obtaining a microwave oven for the first time you will probably not need to buy much in the way of new dishes. All your heat resistant glassware will be suitable and many ordinary china plates etc. (provided they do not have any gold embellishments). No metal containers may be used, but you can put any sort of paper plates in, and even cook on kitchen paper! Round dishes are best because they cook evenly, and better still if you make a hole in the centre — for instance you could put an egg cup in the centre of the dish before filling it — although this is by no means essential.

Many dishes need to be covered to speed up cooking time. For this you will need cling film (always pierced to allow steam to escape, and avoid a 'blow out').

There are now plenty of books available which will give more detailed explanations of how microwave ovens work — but few with suitable wholefood recipes for vegetarians.

If you are using a regular microwave cook book, and converting recipes to wholefoods, my advice would be to add a little more moisture and you may find that the food needs fractionally longer cooking.

The first two editions of this book lacked any pastry and 'proper' bread recipes because they could not be baked without the use of a conventional oven. If you possess a microwave oven you will be able to make successful bread and pastry — although it will not look as good as from an ordinary oven because no browning takes place.

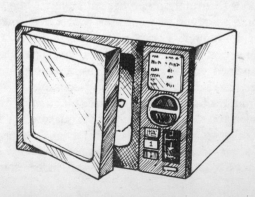

DRYING GARDEN HERBS

Another advantage of a microwave oven is that you can very easily dry your fresh garden herbs. Pick the herbs in the morning on a dry day after any dew has evaporated and before the sun becomes too hot. Then drying them is simplicity itself.

1. Take off any hard stalks, and lay the herbs — a few at a time — on a piece of absorbent paper on the turntable. Heat on full power for 1 minute.

2. Then take them out with the paper and shake them around a little. Return to the oven and heat in 30 second bursts until they feel quite dry — but not too shrivelled.

3. Take them out and set aside for several hours before storing. Store them in dark airtight jars.

CHEESE AND CELERY FLAN

For the pastry:

Imperial (Metric)	American
3 oz (85g) wholemeal flour	¾ cupful wholewheat flour
2 tablespoonsful oatmeal, finely ground	2 tablespoonsful oatmeal, finely ground
1 tablespoonful soya flour	1 tablespoonful soy flour
2 oz (55g) white nut fat or vegetable margarine	¼ cupful white nut fat or vegetable margarine
Water or milk to mix	Water or milk to mix

For the filling:

Imperial (Metric)	American
1 egg	1 egg
¼ pint (140ml) milk	⅔ cupful milk
3 oz (85g) cheese, grated	¾ cupful cheese, grated
Good pinch dry mustard	Good pinch dry mustard
Sea salt and freshly ground black pepper	Sea salt and freshly ground black pepper
2 sticks celery, chopped finely	2 stalks celery, chopped finely
A little extra grated cheese	A little extra grated cheese

1. Make the pastry and line a non-metallic heat-resistant pie dish, prick it well all over. Cook on *full power* for 4 minutes.

2. Mix all filling ingredients in a bowl and pour on to pastry case. Cook on *full power* for 6 minutes. If mixture still looks uncooked in centre give it another minute.

3. Leave to stand for about 10 minutes before serving — it will not need re-heating.

MIXED NUT LOAF

Imperial (Metric)
1 onion, chopped
2 tablespoonsful oil
1 small piece turnip, chopped
1 tomato, skinned and chopped
Large handful fresh herbs including mint, thyme, marjoram, sage or rosemary
4 oz (115g) brown rice, cooked
6 oz (170g) mixed nuts, finely ground
Sea salt and freshly ground black pepper
2 tablespoonsful tomato purée
Good shake *Tabasco*
1 tablespoonful soya sauce
Water or vegetable stock

American
1 onion, chopped
2 tablespoonsful oil
1 small piece turnip, chopped
1 tomato, skinned and chopped
Large handful fresh herbs including mint, thyme, marjoram, sage or rosemary
2/3 cupful brown rice, cooked
1 cupful mixed nuts, finely ground
Sea salt and freshly ground black pepper
2 tablespoonsful tomato paste
Good shake *Tabasco*
1 tablespoonful soy sauce
Water or vegetable stock

1. Put onion and oil into a bowl. Heat for 2 minutes on *full power*.

2. Add the rest of the vegetables and herbs. Heat on *full power* for about 4 minutes or until all is soft.

3. Liquidize or put this through a *mouli*-sieve.

4. Mix all the ingredients together, adding a little water to make a dropping consistency. Allow to stand for about 5 minutes (it will stiffen up a bit). Then put into greased, straight-sided non-metallic dish.

5. Cook for 8-10 minutes on *full power*. Check that the centre is cooked . . . if not return for another 2 minutes or so. Leave for 5-10 minutes before turning out.

MUSHROOM DE LUXE

Imperial (Metric)
4 oz (115g) mushrooms
½ oz (15g) vegetable margarine
1 small onion
Sprigs of basil and thyme, minced
Good pinch of paprika
1 clove garlic
Juice of ½ a lemon

American
2 cupsful mushrooms
1¼ tablespoonsful vegetable
   margarine
1 small onion
Sprigs of basil and thyme, minced
Good pinch of paprika
1 clove garlic
Juice of ½ a lemon

1. Clean the mushrooms by wiping with damp cloth and dry.

2. Put margarine and onion in flattish non-metallic heat-resistant dish and cook on *full power* for 1 minute.

3. Mix in rest of ingredients (except mushrooms). Then put mushrooms in dish, spooning mixture over them. Heat on *full power* for 2-3 minutes. Baste if necessary.

PEANUT PASTA SAVOURY

Imperial (Metric)	American
3 oz (85g) wholewheat macaroni	¾ cupful wholewheat macaroni
¾ pint (425ml) water	2 cupsful water
Sea salt	Sea salt
1 teaspoonful oil	1 teaspoonful oil
2 oz (55g) vegetable margarine	¼ cupful vegetable margarine
2 oz (55g) wholemeal flour	½ cupful wholewheat flour
1 teaspoonful yeast extract	1 teaspoonful yeast extract
1 tablespoonful tomato purée	1 tablespoonful tomato paste
3 oz (85g) peanuts (unsalted), ground	¾ cupful peanuts (unsalted), ground
Oatflakes, sesame seeds or breadcrumbs for coating	Oatflakes, sesame seeds or breadcrumbs for coating

1. To cook macaroni put boiling water with a little salt and a teaspoonful of oil into a large non-metallic heat-resistant container, add macaroni and stir. Cook on *full power* for about 15 minutes or until cooked. Drain and rinse and set aside.

2. Put margarine into a bowl and heat for 1 minute on *full power*.

3. Blend in the flour and gradually add water. Add yeast extract and tomato purée, stir and cook for 1 minute on *full power*, stir and cook for a further minute.

4. Add ground peanuts, then mix in the macaroni and leave to cool.

5. To finish — put the mixture into a shallow, greased serving dish and cook for 5 minutes on *full power*. Brown oatflakes, sesame seeds or breadcrumbs under grill, sprinkle on top and serve.

Note: This mixture can also be shaped and coated with the oatflakes, sesame seeds or breadcrumbs (unbrowned) and fried.

BAKED POTATOES WITH NUT BUTTER

Imperial (Metric)
Even-sized potatoes, 1 for each
person
About 1 good tablespoonful nut
butter per potato

American
Even-sized potatoes, 1 for each
person
About 1 good tablespoonful nut
butter per potato

1. Scrub each potato clean. Pierce with a knife, pat dry in a kitchen cloth and then wrap in a piece of soft kitchen paper.

2. Allow 4 minutes on *full power* for each medium-sized potato. If cooking 3 or 4 at once you can reduce the time by only 2 minutes, i.e., for 3 potatoes allow 10 minutes.

4. When cooked leave (wrapped) for 4 or 5 minutes (they will not cool down quickly).

5. Serve with a generous knob of any of the nut butters (page 41), sprinkled with extra herbs.

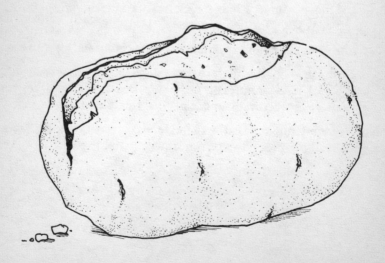

COTTAGE CHEESE AND TOMATO NOODLES

Imperial (Metric)
5 oz (140g) wholewheat noodles
1 tablespoonful margarine
1 small onion, chopped
Sea salt and freshly ground black
   pepper
1 tablespoonful tomato purée
½ teaspoonful paprika
Several leaves fresh basil, chopped
½ lb (225g) cottage cheese
4 tablespoonsful double cream
   (optional)
1 tomato, sliced
A sprinkle of breadcrumbs

American
1 cupful wholewheat noodles
1 tablespoonful margarine
1 small onion, chopped
Sea salt and freshly ground black
   pepper
1 tablespoonful tomato paste
½ teaspoonful paprika
Several leaves fresh basil, chopped
1 cupful cottage cheese
4 tablespoonsful heavy cream
   (optional)
1 tomato, sliced
A sprinkle of breadcrumbs

1. Put noodles into a deep heat-resistant non-metallic dish, add a very good covering of boiling water and heat on *full power* for about 10-15 minutes or until noodles are cooked.

2. Soften margarine in a bowl in oven for 1 minute.

3. Add onions, cook for 2 minutes.

4. Prepare suitable casserole by greasing inside. Mix all ingredients except tomatoes and breadcrumbs.

5. Cook for 3 minutes on *full power*.

6. Spread sliced tomatoes on top, sprinkle with breadcrumbs and brown under the grill.

GNOCCI

Imperial (Metric)	American
½ pint (285ml) milk	1⅓ cupsful milk
2 tablespoonsful butter	2 tablespoonsful butter
Nutmeg	Nutmeg
1½ oz (45g) wholemeal semolina	⅜ cupful wholewheat semolina
2 oz (55g) cheese, grated	½ cupful cheese, grated
1 tablespoonful Parmesan cheese	1 tablespoonful Parmesan cheese
Sea salt and freshly ground black pepper	Sea salt and freshly ground black pepper
Parsley, finely chopped	Parsley, finely chopped

For coating:

Imperial (Metric)	American
Wholemeal flour, egg and breadcrumbs or oatflakes	Wholewheat flour, egg and breadcrumbs or oatflakes
Oil	Oil
Extra parsley for garnish	Extra parsley for garnish

1. Put milk and butter into a large pudding basin and heat on *full power* for 2 minutes.

2. Add grate of nutmeg, sprinkle in semolina, whisking well — return to microwave and heat on *variable power* until thick, whisking every minute.

3. When thickened remove, cool slightly, stir in cheese, seasoning and parsley.

4. Pour onto a wetted surface and leave to cool.

5. Cut into shapes and coat with flour, egg and breadcrumbs or oatflakes.

6. Fry carefully to brown on both sides (using conventional frying pan). Serve with garnish of parsley.

RICE AND WHEAT PILAF

Imperial (Metric)
1 oz (30g) vegetable margarine
4 oz (114g) brown rice
4 oz (115g) whole wheat, soaked
   overnight
1 onion, chopped
1 red pepper, chopped
2 sticks celery, chopped
2 oz (55g) mushrooms, sliced
1 vegetable bouillon cube
½ pint (285ml) water
2 oz (55g) cashew nuts, roughly
   chopped
Parsley

American
2½ tablespoonsful vegetable
   margarine
½ cupful brown rice
½ cupful whole wheat, soaked
   overnight
1 onion, chopped
1 red pepper, chopped
2 stalks celery, chopped
¾ cupful mushrooms, sliced
1 vegetable bouillon cube
1⅓ cupsful water
½ cupful cashew nuts, roughly
   chopped
Parsley

1. Use a deep non-metallic heat-resistant casserole dish.

2. Put in margarine, rice, wheat, onion, red pepper and celery. Heat uncovered on *full power* for 5 minutes.

3. Add rest of ingredients except parsley and cashew nuts. Cover (with lid or film) cook on *simmer* for 25 minutes. Take out and leave to stand for 5 minutes or so — then check if rice is cooked, return for a short time if it is not.

4. Brown nuts under the grill and sprinkle over the top with parsley just before serving.

BORSCHT

Imperial (Metric)
About 1 lb (455g) raw beetroots
1 oz (30g) soya flour
1 pint (570ml) water
1 teaspoonful sea salt
Freshly ground black pepper
1 tablespoonful molasses
Juice of 1 lemon
Good grate nutmeg
Yogurt, sour cream or soya milk

American
About 1 pound raw beet
¼ cupful soy flour
2½ cupful water
1 teaspoonful sea salt
Freshly ground black pepper
1 tablespoonful molasses
Juice of 1 lemon
Good grate nutmeg
Yogurt, sour cream or soy milk

1. Grate the beetroots. Mix soya flour with a little water to a paste thinning with more water, and put into a large non-metallic heat-resistant bowl with all the other ingredients. Stir and cook on *full power*, uncovered, or 10 minutes or until beets are cooked.

2. This can be put through a *mouli*-sieve or not as preferred.

3. It is best eaten cold with a good garnish of yogurt, sour cream or soya milk.

MIXED VEGETABLE SOUP

Imperial (Metric)
1 large onion, chopped
Oil for frying
1 tablespoonful lentils
1 tablespoonful wheat — soaked
  overnight if possible
1 carrot, chopped
1 piece of turnip, chopped
1 stick of celery, chopped
1 vegetable bouillon
Few drops *Tabasco*
Good shake soya sauce
Sea salt and freshly ground black
  pepper
Good pinch nutmeg
Large sprig oregano and mint
½ pint (285ml) water
1 oz (30g) soya flour
Handful of sproutings

American
1 large onion, chopped
Oil for frying
1 tablespoonful lentils
1 tablespoonful wheat — soaked
  overnight if possible
1 carrot, chopped
1 piece of turnip, chopped
1 stalk of celery, chopped
1 vegetable bouillon
Few drops *Tabasco*
Good shake soy sauce
Sea salt and freshly ground black
  pepper
Good pinch nutmeg
Large sprig oregano and mint
1⅓ cupsful water
¼ cupful soy flour
Handful of sproutings

1. Put oil and onions in a large non-metallic heat resistant bowl. Heat on *full power* for 2 minutes.

2. Add lentils and wheat, mix and return to microwave for 1 minute on *full power*.

3. Add all other ingredients except sproutings. Cook covered for 10 minutes on *full power*.

4. At this stage you can liquidize the soup if desired. Add the sproutings and leave them raw or return to microwave for 2 minutes on *full power*. If too thick add some boiling water.

REAL TOMATO SOUP

Imperial (Metric)
1 oz (30g) butter or vegetable
  margarine
1 onion, chopped
1½ lb (680g) tomatoes, chopped
  with skins
1 oz (30g) soya flour
1½ pints (850ml) water or
  vegetable stock
Bay leaf
Large sprig of fresh basil
Sea salt and freshly ground black
  pepper
1 tablespoonful tomato purée
Cream, top of the milk or soya milk

American
2½ tablespoonsful butter or
  vegetable margarine
1 onion, chopped
1½ pounds tomatoes, chopped with
  skins
¼ cupful soy flour
3¾ cupsful water or vegetable stock
Bay leaf
Large sprig of fresh basil
Sea salt and freshly ground black
  pepper
1 tablespoonful tomato paste
Cream, top of the milk or soy milk

1. Put margarine and onions in a large non-metallic heat-resistant bowl. Heat on *full power* for 2 minutes.

2. Add tomatoes, mix and heat on *full power* for another 5 minutes, stir several times in between.

3. Mix soya flour with a little water to a paste, thinning with more water, add it and all the other ingredients (except top of milk) to tomatoes, stir and heat uncovered on *full power* for 10 minutes.

4. Put through a *mouli*-sieve, add cream, top of milk or soy milk. Heat in individual bowls for 1 minute.

BASIC CAKE

Imperial (Metric)
6 oz (170g) soft vegetable
   margarine
6 oz (170g) raw cane sugar
6 oz (170g) self-raising wholemeal
   flour
½ teaspoonful baking powder
Few drops vanilla essence
About 4 tablespoonsful milk

American
⅔ cupful soft vegetable margarine
1 cupful raw cane sugar
1½ cupsful self-raising wholewheat
   flour
½ teaspoonful baking powder
Few drops vanilla essence
About 4 tablespoonsful milk

1. Mix all ingredients together in a bowl. For best results use an electric mixer for 2 minutes.

2. Transfer to a greased non-metallic heat-resistant container. Cook on *full power* for 6-7 minutes. The cake will rise quite a lot. You can check and if there is uncooked mixture in the middle heat for another ½ minute.

3. Take out and cover with a paper towel and leave to stand for 5-10 minutes before turning out.

4. Decorate with a sprinkle of sugar or a tablespoonful of chopped almonds.

Variations: Because a microwave oven does not brown food, your cake will not look as good as when cooked in a conventional oven. Chocolate cakes seem to look best, and so a variation would be to add 1 or 2 tablespoonsful carob powder to the mixture, and grate a carob chocolate bar on top while cake is still warm. This basic mixture can also be used for small cakes. It is a good idea to use double paper cases. Cook only 4 or 5 at a time, putting them round the outside of the turntable. They will only take about 1½ minutes.

HONEY AND DATE CRUNCH

Imperial (Metric)	**American**
Juice of ½ a lemon	Juice of ½ a lemon
1 tablespoonful wholemeal flour	1 tablespoonful wholewheat flour
5 oz (140g) dates, stoned and chopped	1 cupful dates, stoned and chopped
3 tablespoonsful honey	3 tablespoonsful honey
8 tablespoonsful water	8 tablespoonsful water
6 oz (170g) vegetable margarine	⅔ cupful vegetable margarine
4 oz (115g) wholemeal flour	1 cupful wholewheat flour
4 oz (115g) raw cane sugar	⅔ cupful raw cane sugar
5 oz (140g) rolled oats	1¼ cupsful rolled oats

1. Grease and line a non-metallic heat-resistant dish (pie plate or square).

2. Mix lemon juice and 1 tablespoonful flour in a small bowl, add dates, honey and 8 tablespoonsful water, stir and cook on *full power* for 2 minutes. Set aside to cool.

3. Put margarine into a larger bowl, heat on *full power* for ½ a minute. Add all rest of ingredients and mix well.

4. Spread half over prepared dish, cover with date mixture, and then press rest over.

5. Cook on *full power* for 5 minutes. Check and return for another minute if very soft in the centre — but the Honey and Date Crunch will continue to cook when it comes out of the microwave.

BAKED APPLES

Imperial (Metric)	American
4 large cooking apples	4 large cooking apples
2 oz (55g) raw cane sugar or honey	1/3 cupful raw cane sugar or honey
2 oz (55g) sultanas or raisins	1/3 cupful golden seedless raisins or raisins
Several dates, chopped	Several dates, chopped
1 tablespoonful cinnamon	1 tablespoonful cinnamon
Grated nutmeg	Grated nutmeg
A little lemon juice	A little lemon juice
Water	Water

1. Wipe apples and gently score right round the centre with a sharp knife. Take out cores and place the apples together on flat non-metallic dish.

2. Mix all ingredients except water together in a bowl and put spoonsful into the holes. If there is some over (this will depend on size of apples) you can put it into the base of the dish. Otherwise put just 2 or 3 tablespoonsful of water in the dish. Heat on *full power* for 3 to 4 minutes. Allow to stand for 5 minutes before serving.

WHOLEMEAL BREAD

Imperial (Metric)
1 teaspoonful raw cane sugar
1 level teaspoonful dried yeast
½ pint (285ml) water
15 oz (425g) wholemeal flour
1 oz (30g) soya flour
A little sea salt

American
1 teaspoonful raw cane sugar
1 level teaspoonful dried yeast
1⅓ cupsful water
Just under 4 cupsful wholewheat
    flour
¼ cupful soy flour
A little sea salt

1. In a small bowl put sugar, yeast and about ⅓ of the water. Warm on *full power* for 30 seconds. Stir and leave to stand for about 8 minutes.

2. Meanwhile mix flours and sea salt. If flour is cold you can warm on *full power* for 15 seconds.

3. When yeast has risen add it to flours with remaining water (which has been warmed), mix well, and turn out and knead for a few moments. Shape and put into a suitable greased container.

4. Leave in a warm place (inside a plastic bag helps to speed rising). You can also put into microwave on *defrosting setting* for 30 seconds every 5 minutes or so to speed up.

5. Cook on *roast (or variable heat)* for 10 minutes. The bread will not look cooked and you can place it under a hot grill for a few minutes to crispen and slightly colour the crust.

Note: An even simpler way of breadmaking is to use a yeast that can be put straight into the flour. I use *Fermipan* which is sold in vacuum packed bags, and is very economical as one needs less than ordinary dried yeast.

INDEX